Table Talk

Table Talk

Resources for
the Communion Meal

Edited by
Jane McAvoy

Chalice Press
St. Louis, Missouri

Cover Artwork: Kim Yong Gil
Courtesy of Asian Christian Art Association, Kyoto, Japan

Art Director: Michael Dominguez

Library of Congress Cataloging–in–Publication Data

Table talk: resources for the communion meal/ edited by Jane E. McAvoy.
    Includes bibliographical references.
    ISBN 0-8272-3632-8
    1. Lord's Supper   I. McAvoy, Jane Ellen, 1957–
BV825.2.T235 1993   264'.36   93-12110

Acknowledgments

A communion of voices is present in this collection. I am grateful to the individuals who submitted materials for this volume. Their writing underscores the diversity and vitality of contemporary Christian worship. Two other individuals who were central to this project are David Polk, editor of Chalice Press, and Millie Schwan, faculty secretary at Hiram College. For their interest in this project and their hard work, I give thanks.

Jane McAvoy
Christmas, 1992

Contents

The Table
That Talks to Us

Once, the communion table talked to me. In the midst of meditative contemplation, a clear voice came to me, saying, "Jane, you forgot to put the roast in the oven." This proclamation raised me from my slumber. For the rest of communion—in fact, for the rest of the entire worship service—I meditated not on the mystery of salvation but on the miracles of the microwave.

I recount this experience of table talk with more than a little embarrassment. As a minister and theologian I have spent hours thinking about the mystery of communion and its revelation of the God who communes with us. Yet on this ordinary Sunday morning my thoughts were consumed with the preparation of an ordinary Sunday meal. Thoughts of the sacred lost out to the reality of the mundane.

This book is written with the conviction that my experience is not unique. Week after week the Christian community comes to the table with reverent hearts hoping to contemplate the mysteries of faith, but is distracted by the realities of everyday life. The mysterious presence of bread and wine is overshadowed by the presence of concrete realities and struggles from the trivial to the tragic. The problem is not that we are irreverent, but rather that the words we hear at the table do not relate to the complexities of our lives. What we experience is a conflict between "the gentle religious ritual and the harsh life that people are forced to live outside of the safety of church walls and ceremonies" (Watkins 83*). The table does not talk to us.

The irony is that the very act we celebrate around the communion table is a profound testimony to God's encounter with the world in all its trials and tribulations. The communion table proclaims the saving activity of God revealed in Jesus Christ. It is a celebration of God's transforming power and profound presence. "This is my body; this is my blood," proclaims the mystery of the God who communes with us. If the table is to talk to us, we must look beneath the observance of communion and contemplate the mystery that this act remembers.

This Is My Body: The Mystery of God's Presence

Many congregations live by the motto, "When we meet, we eat." The image that this generally brings to mind is the fellowship dinner or coffee hour after worship, filled with friendly conversation. It is a time for building relationships, sharing joys and sorrows, and taking part in the social reality of the church. Underneath this motto is the wisdom that through the act of eating together we are nourished as individuals and as the church.

When we meet around the communion table we eat the bread that has been understood throughout Christian tradition to be nourishment for the soul (Sykes 280). It is bread that remembers the body lived with us, lived for us. It symbolizes the powerful presence of God. It is the liberating presence of a God who breaks barriers against injustice, freeing Israel from oppression and abiding with them as a pillar of fire by night and as a cloud by day. It is the redeeming presence that is embodied in Jesus' servanthood of mutual relation with all people—from the Samaritan woman to the tax collector Zacchaeus. It is an abiding presence that continues in those

*For publishing information on works cited, see p. 127.

such as Mary Magdalene who grasp Jesus' vision of a realm of inclusion in which all live in harmony.

But the mystery of this bread is that it symbolizes a broken presence. It is powerful in its promise to abide with us into the depths of our lives. It is a presence that has experienced the depths of human despair, crying, "My God, my God, why have you forsaken me?" It is a perplexing presence that does not abandon suffering. It is a mystery that embraces "death, sin and all forms of alienation for the sake of life" (LaCugna, *God for Us* 1). It is not the presence of a triumphant king who passes on his rule first through a heavenly Son and subsequently through a divinely appointed court of male priests. It is rather the scandalous presence of an illegitimate son, who comes in the form of a slave (Schaberg). By embracing humanity through the form of the "lowest of the low," this son embraces all.

As Marjorie Proctor-Smith notes, to remember this presence is not a painless process. It calls for acts of both thanksgiving and lament: lament for suffering and death and thanksgiving for life, health, and liberation (Proctor-Smith 38, 263). In this sense, to remember is a courageous act. It is to confront honestly a God who suffers, and to name the suffering of our world. It calls us to confront the pain of our lives and to dare to bring this pain to the communion meal. Its hope is that through this breaking of bread "communion becomes a profound source of energy for the healing of suffering. Knowing we are not abandoned makes all the difference" (Johnson 267).

This is a truth that is known by every women's fellowship group that faithfully prepares a meal for the grieving family following a funeral. In these moments the motto, "When we meet, we eat," takes on a new meaning, for it proclaims that we meet in every moment of our lives, even in our suffering, as the church in the presence of God.

This Is My Blood: The Mystery of God's Power

An old gospel hymn proclaims, "There's power, power, wonder-working power in the precious blood of the lamb." The words are punctuated by a pulsating beat that can inspire a congregation to fill the rafters with energetic singing. Music weaves in and around the lungs of young and old, filling them with life and joining them together into one voice of praise.

This is my blood are words about the present power of God
that is the life-force flowing through the veins of our lives. It is
the juice of the vine that recalls Jesus' proclamation, "I am the
vine, you are the branches" (John 15:5). It symbolizes the
present power of God. It is the power of relation, the power of
a God who declares, "You shall be my people, and I will be
your God." It is the reciprocal power of Jesus, whose healing
power flows to the bleeding woman through her touch. It is
the power that continues in our midst where two or three are
gathered together by the passion of the gospel. It is a transforming power that, by flowing between and among all of
creation, is larger than the sum of its parts.

The mystery of this cup is that it proclaims the agony of
shed blood. At the communion table we are confronted with
the paradox of a present power. It talks to us of divine sacrifice that challenges our understanding of God's activity in the
world. The mystery of the gospel does not portray God's control *over* creation. Rather it unveils divine power acting *in and
through* creation. It is the power of God that can be thwarted
by an obstinate people who follow kings instead of Yahweh,
who mistake a kingdom of earthly possessions for a reign of
peace and goodwill. It is a power that abides with women who
endure oppression, abuse, and rape at the hands of those with
whom they have entered into relation. It is a belief in a
persistent power that continues to work for justice in spite of
the crucifixion of Jesus and the continuing crucifixions of our
daily lives.

It is hard to remain true to this mystery. Too often our
communion prayers deny this mystery by proclaiming Jesus'
sacrifice as an end in itself, and divine power as "the force that
could stop all of this suffering but simply chooses not to, for
whatever reason." (Johnson 249). This understanding rein-
forces the false impression that God's power is coercive and
even intrusive (Wilson-Kastner 99). Rita Brock declares this
theology to be nothing more than a proclamation of "cosmic
child abuse" (Brock 56).

To proclaim the present power of God requires an honest
confrontation with the meaning of Jesus' sacrifice as a tragic
means to the end of remaining true to the radical power of
mutuality. As Beverly Harrison explains, "Jesus was radical
not in his lust for sacrifice but in his power of mutuality....To
be sure, Jesus was faithful unto death....But his sacrifice was

for the cause of radical love, to make relationship and to sustain it, and above all, to right wrong relationship" (Harrison 18–19).

The communion table speaks to us of precious blood that has the wonder-working power to remain in relation with us into and through the depths of our lives. To name this power honestly requires us to reinterpret sacrifice as a communal act of discernment, calling the Christian community to work for the sacrifice of unjust power in our church and in our world (Proctor-Smith 162). As we lift the communion cup we may indeed "see in a mirror, dimly," but we do see God's present power given for us, given to us.

Talk at the Table

Those who lead the Christian community have the privilege and responsibility to lead the congregation in the act of remembering the mystery of broken bread and shed blood. Communion prayers must not be afraid to name the pain of remembering the presence that suffers with the world or the joy of celebrating the power that works through the world. By naming the reality of suffering and struggling to comprehend sacrifice within a framework of God's communion with the world, the prayers and meditations around the communion table will indeed talk to us.

In the chapters that follow, you will find a collection of meditations, prayers, and litanies that show how reflection on the mystery of communion can revive our talk around the table. Central to these resources is contemplation on the mystery of God's body broken for us; God's blood shed for us. The resources show the diversity of the Christian community joined together by the courageous act of remembrance and the prophetic vision of imagination.

These resources are gathered together around the seasons of the liturgical year. As God's power and presence are active in the world in a multitude of ways, so the point of the liturgical year is to celebrate this diversity of activity and to be challenged by the mystery of God's power and presence. "In the course of a single year the worshiping church relives the entire drama of salvation history through a continual remembrance of God's redemptive acts on our behalf" (LaCugna, *God for Us* 406).

Thus, as communion is celebrated throughout the liturgical year, certain nuances of this multifaceted activity are highlighted. The year begins with Advent, a season that proclaims the hope of God's power to be present in the world. In Christmastide the community grows in the power of God's presence. During Lent Christians struggle with the reality of God's present power. Easter erupts with the celebration of the power of God's presence. The liturgical year ends with the long season of Pentecost, a sharing in the presence of God's power, until once again we are recalled to the hope of the Advent season.

These resources have been written by a variety of worship leaders who have given their permission for you to utilize their work. Initials are provided in parentheses after each item to indicate the source of that contribution, with the key to those initials given at the back of the book.

As you use this book, you will find that communion meditations are often combined with appropriate communion prayers. Often these materials were composed by one person, as a unit. But in other cases, meditations and prayers by different individuals have been brought together because of a common theme. You may find some of those combinations more suitable than others. And that's fine.

The hope of all of us who have contributed to this volume is that this collection will assist you in communion preparation. These resources are provided to aid pastors and elders with communion meditations and prayers in a wide variety of ways, and to aid worship participants in their private meditations and their understanding of communion.

This collection is also offered to inspire your own meditation on the themes of communion throughout the various seasons of the year. May your imagination be sparked by these resources, and may they inspire you to compose your own reflections on the mystery of communion. As you commune with these voices from the Christian community, may the table talk to you.

Advent

Proclaiming the Hope of God's Power to Be Present in the World

Decorating for Christmas is a big deal at my house. Every year we put up the tree that my husband's family bought when he was a teenager. Every year the tree loses a few more branches and reveals a few more holes. Every year we consider throwing it away. But we can never quite bring ourselves to do it. The tree has seen twenty-five Advent seasons. It is filled with childhood memories for my husband. Throughout the years of our marriage it has taken on an even greater importance as a symbol of the way we have merged memories and families so that now it is truly our tree. This became clear to me this year, when I was the one arguing for the tree when he wanted to throw it out.

Each year, after our ritual debate over the future of the tree, we decide once again to accept the challenge of transforming that bedraggled heap of plastic into our Christmas tree. It usually takes all day. For one thing, we are supposed to wash the tree every year. Then my husband painstakingly weaves strands of tiny colored lights through the fragile branches. Finally it is time to decorate. Diplomatic decisions are made about which old ornaments must be thrown away and where our newest acquisitions will be hung. When we start decorating we merely hope that it will not look too shabby. But slowly the tree is transformed until it is not merely presentable, but is even magnificent. When all the decorations are arranged we sit on the couch, turn off the other lights in the house, and spend a few magical moments in silence, surrounded by memories of the past beckoning us to dream toward the future.

Advent is the season of expectation for the future, built on past remembrance of God's action in the world and present needs for God's redeeming power. It requires hope for the future that is not blind faith but memorable faith. It hopes that the God who ransomed captive Israel, who was present in the death of Jesus, is still Emmanuel: God with us. No matter what our circumstances, no matter what the situation of the world, celebrating communion during Advent is an expectant act that proclaims God's power to be present in the world. It is a few magical moments of silence surrounded by memories of the past, beckoning us to dream toward the future.

1. Meditation and Prayer

We busy ourselves these days with many things: buying gifts, mailing cards, getting ready for the party, deciding what to wear for the wedding. Are the pets in? Where are my winter gloves? And in the midst of it, we suddenly find ourselves here, at the table, in the presence of the Lord—the word become flesh, the bread become the body, the wine the blood. Suddenly, in the midst of the daily activity of our lives, we are confronted again with the truth that God loves us so much the Holy One came to be a part of our daily lives as a child—a teacher—as God incarnate and to come again in bread and wine. We rejoice.

(CDN)

(Luke 1:67–79)
Prayer for the Bread and Cup:
Merciful God, we, like Zechariah, long to be freed from our silence so that we might raise our voices in proclamation of your mighty acts of love in our lives. May this bread strengthen us to be beacons of light to those who sit in darkness. May this cup pour over us with saving grace so that we might proclaim the knowledge of salvation to your people. In this communion may the advent of your presence dawn in our lives. Amen.

(JM)

2. Responsive Reading and Prayer

Leader: In the beginning God created all things and saw that they were good.

People: OUR HOPE IS THAT GOD'S GOOD CREATION ENDURES FOREVER.

Leader: God sought a special relationship with the humanity of creation.

People: OUR HOPE IS THAT BY WALKING WITH GOD, LIKE ABRAHAM AND SARAH, WE, TOO, WILL BLESS THE EARTH.

Leader: God has taught each generation with the old Word and with new words.

People: OUR HOPE IS TO RECOGNIZE GOD'S PROPHETS IN OUR DAY, TO PURSUE COURAGEOUSLY GOD'S WILL FOR OUR LIVES.

Leader: God established a new covenant, and Love incarnate emerged from a manger bed.

People: OUR HOPE IS TO BELIEVE, FOR WE HAVE SEEN GOD WITH EYES OF FAITH...TO TRUST, FOR GOD IS FAITHFUL...TO DO THE WORK OF FAITH, FOR WE ARE STEWARDS OF GOD'S CREATION AND COVENANT.

Leader: The life, death, and resurrection of Jesus Christ we celebrate with bread and wine.

People: WE PROCLAIM OUR HOPE IN GOD'S POWER TO GIVE LIFE, TO RENEW LIFE, AND TO BESTOW LIFE EVERLASTING.

Prayer for Communion:

God of history, in thankful praise we retell the story our forebears in the faith have lived and told. In our remembering we are drawn closer into the infinite circle of your love. With joyful hopefulness we come to partake of the symbols of that communion.

In eating of this loaf and drinking from this cup, we pray for unity in the body represented here. We pray for forgiveness in the blood of Jesus consecrated here. Renew our spirits and strengthen our hands for courageous ministry. God of history, we live in your kingdom and anticipate in hope its coming in fullness.

Through Jesus Christ, who became flesh as we are flesh and reigns with you forever. Amen.

(MAP)

3. A Prayer for the Cup
(Based on *Donkey's Dream*)

The donkey shambles in the night
toward Bethlehem,
bearing a rose
whose petals will soon open.

This cup holding its elemental liquid
means many things to us,
O God of the mother's embrace,
but never more than in this season
do we know it as the womb
of the divine;
Before the new man
can shed his blood for us,
a woman must shed hers
for him.

The rose will open,
its petals fall;
suddenly, we will see the thorns;
and know that this moment of birth
is one
with the moment of death.

In awe of the miracle of life,
we rejoice in this Advent,
merciful Mother,
for in your humanity,
we will find our own.

We come now to your table with hearts open
and full of the good news!

(CC)

4. Communion Prayer
(Luke 3:16)

Dear Jesus, we remember that John the Baptist said that while he baptized with water, you would baptize with the Holy Spirit and with fire. May we know that baptism of fire that your Spirit may burn within us, that we shall have a new heart and life.

As we participate in this holy communion,

light in us your baptism of fire, that the blaze of that flame will illuminate the dark corners of our souls and be a beacon to lead us to your truth;

kindle in us your baptism of fire, that the warmth of that fire may warm our hearts with love for you and for each other;

ignite in us your baptism of fire, that its purifying flame will burn away all that is false in us and leave that which is true.

Like the refiner's fire, cleanse us and make us pure, that we may live in your spiritual kingdom and that you may abide in us and we in you. Amen.

(KT)

5. Meditation and Prayer
(Luke 2:22–38)

During this season we gather around the table often with friends, with colleagues, with family. In the midst of our busy lives we savor the taste of family recipes passed down from generation to generation. We are delighted by the smell of fresh-cut greens. We delight in the sound of children sweetly singing. We rejoice in the beauty of freshly fallen snow.

This is the season of joy, when the prophet Anna saw the Christ Child and began to proclaim good news to all who were looking for redemption. As we gather around this table, her words continue to echo in the hearts of all those looking for redemption. Let us partake of this meal and rejoice.

Prayer:

With joy-filled hearts we come, O God, to this communion table. Like Anna, we recognize the beauty of new life in our midst, the wonder of your grace in those who celebrate with us the joys of life. As we celebrate this feast of bread and cup, may we, like Simeon, see with our own eyes your salvation, which you have prepared in the presence of all peoples. May we rise from this table to shine as a light to all the nations, a joy to the world. Amen.

(JM)

6. Meditation and Prayer

Danger lurks in our celebrations of the Advent season, from our carols about the meek baby Jesus and his mild mother Mary to our tender memories of Christmas past. "O Come, O Come, Emmanuel," we sing, thinking only of the birth of a baby whose remembered arrival barely disturbs our pleasant present. That danger bursts into full threat whenever we believe, consciously or unconsciously, that Advent is a season for looking backwards to a long ago birth in faraway Bethlehem. For in such times we ignore another coming, a future coming, of our Lord and another birth, our own birth, into God's eternal reign.

Our present-day lectionaries reveal awareness of this danger. Included in every set of readings for the first Sunday in Advent is a gospel reading, taken not from the opening chapters of the Gospels about the first arrival of Jesus, but from the last chapters in which Jesus offers warnings about another arrival. There will be, he says to his disciples, times of great trauma and stress; receive them as labor pains signaling the impending advent of the Son of Man. And keep awake, for no one knows the day or the hour when he will come.

Too often, however, we lull ourselves to sleep with strains of "Silent Night, Holy Night." We seem blissfully unaware that Advent is the season for waiting and preparing not just for the Christ Child, but for Christ the Ruler of the Cosmos. It is, after all, much simpler to cling to a pious remembrance of a happy moment in history than to hold fast to a hope in a dim, unknowable future.

At the table of our Lord, a wake-up tug is offered as we remember that Jesus' birth is prelude to Jesus' death and resurrection. Snapped back to attention, we remind ourselves that Jesus' birth into this world is a foreshadowing of our own birth into God's ultimate reign. Around this table we look not only backwards to the gentle advent of a baby, but also forward toward a future in which that baby, the crucified and resurrected one, will bring us into communion with the God of all creation's destiny.

(NCP)

(Mark 13:32–37)
Prayer for the Bread:

Alpha and Omega, we come into your everlasting presence this day. This bread, symbol of your life with us, is leaven in our lives. It fills us with the memory of suffering endured for the sake of the world. It nourishes our longing for acceptance, for meaning, for fulfilling life. May it strengthen us ever to keep alert for the door that opens to your ever-coming realm. Amen.

Prayer for the Cup:

Master, as we drink this cup, may it awaken us from the slumber of our lives lived in the obligations of this Advent season. Refreshed, may we awaken to the expectant hope of your presence in our midst. Revived, may we keep alert so that, like the doorkeeper, we may be able to recognize you upon your return. Amen.

(JM)

7. Litany for Communion

Leader: Our lives cry out for a Savior.
We wait and watch, O God,
our Hope and our Salvation.

Right: CHILDREN ARE ROBBED OF THEIR CHILDHOOD.
THE OLD ONES LIVE IN POVERTY AND ISOLATION.
LIVES ARE DEGRADED, USED UP, THROWN AWAY.
OUR RELATIONSHIPS ARE WITHOUT JOY.

Leader: Our lives cry out for a Savior.
We wait and watch, O God,
our Hope and our Salvation.

Left: WOMEN, MEN, AND CHILDREN DIE OF STARVATION.
CANCER AND AIDS RAVAGE OUR LIVES.
WE ARE ADDICTED AND AFRAID.
VIOLENCE HAS BECOME A WAY OF LIFE.

All: OUR LIVES CRY OUT FOR A SAVIOR.
GATHER US, O GOD,
AROUND THE TABLE OF HOPE AND SALVATION.
OPEN OUR HEARTS TO EXPECT THE PRESENCE OF THE CHRIST.
CLEAR OUR PATH TO THE WAY OF SAVING LOVE.
IN THIS BREAD, BREAK OPEN FOR US THE GRAIN OF NEW LIFE.
WITH THIS CUP, POUR OUT YOUR SALVATION FOR ALL.
IN COMMUNION WITH CHRIST AND WITH ONE ANOTHER, MAY
WE CLAIM YOUR POWER COMING INTO THE WORLD. AMEN.

(JF)

8. Communion Liturgy

The Great Thanksgiving:

Leader: May God be with you.

People: AND ALSO WITH YOU.

Leader: Lift up your hearts.

People: WE LIFT THEM UP TO GOD.

Leader: Let us give thanks to God.

People: IT IS RIGHT TO GIVE GOD THANKS AND PRAISE.

Leader: God of eternity, God of history: in the time before time, you were. In an act of love and self-giving, you made order out of chaos and created all that is: the universe, this earth, its life, and humankind. In your generosity you gave to us all you had created. Therefore we raise to you this song of praise and thanksgiving, sung throughout the ages of human history, and in every corner of eternal heaven:

People: HOLY, HOLY, HOLY LORD, GOD OF POWER AND MIGHT, HEAVEN AND EARTH ARE FULL OF YOUR GLORY.
HOSANNA IN THE HIGHEST.
BLESSED IS HE WHO COMES IN THE NAME OF THE LORD.
HOSANNA IN THE HIGHEST.

Leader: Rejected God: in the midst of abundance, we turned away from you and your gifts and created idols for our hardened hearts. But your love has no limits, and so in the fullness of time you sent to us the greatest gift known to all eternity: your only Son, Jesus, the Christ. He came and pitched his tent among us, to live and die as humans must. But his death was that of an innocent. Even in the midst of shame and betrayal, he showed his love for us.

Words of Institution:

People: AS OFTEN AS WE EAT THIS BREAD AND DRINK THE CUP, WE PROCLAIM THE LORD'S DEATH UNTIL HE COMES.

Leader: And so we cry out the joy of our faith:

People: CHRIST HAS DIED.
CHRIST IS RISEN.
CHRIST WILL COME AGAIN.

Leader: We celebrate these holy acts that brought us to redemption, and wait impatiently for your Son to return to us again.

People: MARANATHA!
COME, LORD JESUS, COME!
WE NEED YOU HERE;
WE NEED YOU NOW.
COME, LORD JESUS, COME!
MARANATHA!

Leader: We offer you these gifts, O giver of all, and ask that you would send your Holy Spirit upon them, that they would be for us the body and blood of your Son, our Savior, Jesus Christ. And send your Spirit upon us, we pray, that we would receive the presence of your son in these humble elements of bread and cup, and go, accompanied by him, into the world.

People: EMMANUEL! HE IS WITH US!

Leader: All this we ask in the name of your Son, Jesus Christ. By him, and with him, and in him, in the unity of the Holy Spirit, all honor and glory are yours, almighty God our Father and Mother, now and forever.

People: AMEN.

The Lord's Prayer
Communion
Prayer After Communion:

Leader: Let us pray.

People: GOD OF ALL GENEROSITY,
WE THANK YOU FOR YOUR GIFTS:
FOR YOUR SON, JESUS CHRIST,
THE NOURISHMENT OF HIS BODY AND BLOOD,
AND FOR HIS PRESENCE WITH US NOW.
SEND US OUT INTO THE WORLD
ACCOMPANIED BY CHRIST,
TO TAKE HIS PRESENCE
TO THOSE WHO WAIT WITHOUT THE HOPE
YOU HAVE GIVEN US TODAY.
IN THE NAME OF YOUR SON, JESUS CHRIST, WE PRAY. AMEN.

(KLS)

9. Litany for Communion

Pastor: The Lord be with you.

People: AND ALSO WITH YOU.

Pastor: Lift up your hearts.

People: WE LIFT THEM UP TO THE LORD.

Pastor: Let us give thanks to the Lord our God.

People: IT IS RIGHT TO GIVE THANKS AND PRAISE.

Pastor: It is right, and a good and joyful thing, always and everywhere to give thanks to you, Lord God Almighty, Creator of heaven and earth.

Elder 1:   Especially in this time of waiting, it is good to give thanks to you. Throughout the ages, as your people have waited to hear your voice, you have spoken to them through prophets and rulers, through creation and the Holy Spirit.

People: LORD, WE ARE WAITING.

Elder 2:   In times of bondage and oppression, you spoke words of liberation and freedom. In times of prosperity and self-reliance, you spoke words of challenge and self-denial. In the in-between times, between the already and the not yet, you speak words of patience and endurance, steadfastness and assurance. And we remember your promise:

People: THOSE WHO WAIT FOR THE LORD SHALL RENEW THEIR STRENGTH, THEY SHALL MOUNT UP WITH WINGS LIKE EAGLES (Isaiah 40:31).

Elder 1:   In the midst of this waiting time, you offer to us symbols of your promise, reminders of your presence, and promises for your future. In the bread and in the cup, we find hope in the memory of our Lord, who in his obedience to you faced even the cross and received the resurrection. And in these simple gifts, we celebrate too the promise for the future, of the day when Christ will eat again with us in the kingdom of God. In this bread, and in this cup, we are strengthened not only by our memories of the past, but of our hope for the future.

Elder 2: Pour out your Spirit now on these elements: upon the bread, and upon the cup. May they be for us more than a reminder of the past, but a foretaste of the future. As we eat of this bread and drink of this cup, may our lives bear witness to the kingdom of God that has already come but is not yet fully realized.

People: WE GIVE THANKS FOR THESE GIFTS, UNDESERVED YET GRATEFULLY RECEIVED, AND WE LOOK FORWARD WITH LONGING TO THE TIME WHEN WE, AND ALL CHRISTIANS, WILL JOIN CHRIST AS HIS TABLE IN THE KINGDOM OF GOD. IN JESUS' NAME WE PRAY. AMEN.

(SM)

10. Prayers for Bread and Cup
(Isaiah 61; John 1)

Prayer for the Bread:

Bread of Life, we gather around this table today rejoicing in your righteousness that shoots forth from this meal. As we share this bread, may we be nourished by the good news that binds up the brokenhearted, proclaims liberty to the captives, and release to the prisoners. May praise be implanted in our hearts and vision in our minds so that we may spring forth from this table proclaiming the year of your favor. Amen.

Prayer for the Cup:

Light of the World, we gather around this table today rejoicing in your truth that sparkles in this cup. As the prophets of old, we look into the dimness of our world with the expectant hope of your reign of justice and peace. We cling to the promise that blood spilled in violence will not endure. May we rise from this table prepared to make straight the way of the Lord. Amen.

(JM)

11. Litany for Communion

One: In the name of Jesus, you are invited to gather at this table, where God's living Word offers us food and drink to nourish our spirits.

All: AS JESUS KNEW WE DO NOT LIVE BY BREAD ALONE, WE RECOGNIZE OUR NEED FOR THE LIFE-GIVING WORD OF GOD.

One: We rejoice that in Jesus, God's Word became flesh and chose to dwell in our midst.

All: WE REJOICE THAT JESUS CAME TO REVEAL GOD'S LOVE TO US AND OFFER US THE GIFT OF A NEW RELATIONSHIP WITH GOD.

One: Through the simple elements of bread and wine, Jesus linked our hunger for physical food with our need for spiritual food and offered us a new way of celebrating and experiencing God's love.

All: AS WE SHARE THIS COMMUNION MEAL, WE KNOW GOD'S PRESENCE IN A VERY PERSONAL WAY. WE ARE UNITED WITH GOD AND WITH ONE ANOTHER, NOT ONLY IN THIS PLACE AND TIME, BUT WITH THE FAITHFUL ONES WHO HAVE FOLLOWED CHRIST IN ALL TIMES AND PLACES.

One: Jesus taught that the broken bread was a sign of his broken body.

All: WE REMEMBER THAT HIS BODY WAS INDEED BROKEN.

One: Likewise, this cup is a sign of his blood shed for us all.

All: WE REMEMBER THE GREAT PRICE JESUS PAID FOR OUR REDEMPTION FROM SIN AND DEATH.

One: Emmanuel, the Promised One, God-with-us, has come to dwell among us. As we come to this table, Emmanuel is indeed in our midst.

All: WE REJOICE AS WE EAT THIS BREAD AND DRINK THIS WINE [CUP] TOGETHER BECAUSE WE KNOW GOD'S LOVE FOR US.

One: May God-with-us remind us what love requires of us as we continue to live and grow together as God's people.

All: MAY WE SPREAD THE GOOD NEWS OF PEACE ON EARTH AND GOODWILL TO ALL THAT IS PART OF GOD'S BELOVED CREATION.

(AP)

12. Meditation and Prayer

From my first days as a staff member on a college campus, I learned that the best way to work with students is to feed them. They are always hungry, they are always poor (or so they say), and they hate dorm or cafeteria food. A good home-cooked meal warms their hearts, opens their minds, and fills them body and soul with your best intentions and your most creative expressions of nourishment.

On one occasion of providing a feast of barbecued ribs and fixins for a group of Kappa Sigmas (hearty eaters), these young men opened up and began sharing their concerns and struggles between bites of potato salad and garlic bread. Each in turn began to share the horror of their sophomore year during cleanup week, just before school started, when there was a fire in the fraternity house. The house burned, and four boys had died in the fire. These young men emerging from adolescence had not previously dealt with death, or immortality, or the loss of important persons in their young lives. I watched and listened as they devoured pounds of ribs and homemade sauce, and a huge bowl of potato salad. The more they ate, the more they opened up and shared the fears and memories of the most frightening time in their lives.

One young man, nicknamed "Shylo," was very silent, though not the least bit reticent about eating. Finally, someone confronted him head-on. "Hey, man, you're awfully quiet! Don't you have any thoughts or feelings on this fire? After all, it was you that lost your brother in the fire." Aside from enthusiastic gastronomical sounds, the group of seven or eight was quiet, waiting for "Shylo" to respond. He sat for a moment, thinking and trying to make peace with the painful memory of the loss of the person that he had loved the most in his life, his older brother. Finally, "Shylo" spoke. "I always felt guilty, you know. We called Mom and Dad and they came as quickly as they could. I stood outside the charred ruins of the frat house, knowing that my brother was dead, and I felt ashamed and guilty to be alive. My folks were kind of in shock when they arrived and they never really said too much. I just felt guilty standing there alive and untouched when my brother was dead."

I responded to "Shylo," "Did you ever think about the fact that your parents had sustained a great loss in the death of your brother, but also had a sense of relief when they saw you alive and well and there to greet them as you all proceeded to deal with a very painful loss? Did you ever imagine that they would have been devastated and hopeless had they lost both of their sons? Did you not imagine what a gift it was to them when they saw you alive and well and healthy?"

Silence.

"Shylo" responded, "I never thought of that; I never thought of my life as a gift to my parents....Thanks." He went back with a new spirit to his meal.

In all times, in all ways, in all of our days, when we are willing and open and ready, the Holy Spirit enters in, and we are always deserving. "He had made known to them in the breaking of the bread" (Luke 24:35b).

Prayer for Communion:

Almighty and Creator God,

We ask you to be with us in this season of hope and peace as we prepare once again for the coming of your Son into our lives and into our world. Remind us at this table that we are called together again and again, week after week, to practice the presence of the Christ in our midst. Even as we await his return, we remember and acknowledge the gift of his life, the gift of renewed life, the gift of eternal life.

Touch our hearts and memories, and nourish us with this cup and this loaf, as we recognize that in our midst is the ever-constant spirit of renewal and forgiveness and hope. Help us to know that each one of us is chosen as a child of your kingdom, worthy of your blessing and gifted with eternal life. Feed and heal us today.

In the name of the Christ we pray. Amen.

(CH)

13. Cradle and Cross

Music:

Soloist/choir sings the Christmas carol "I Wonder as I Wander." The song begins, "I wonder as I wander out under the sky, how Jesus the Savior did come for to die. For poor or'n'ry people like you and like I...."

Optional Dramatic Enactment:
During the music, Mary enters carrying the baby Jesus. Mary walks around the chancel, stopping often to rock Jesus or turn around while holding baby Jesus up high. A robed person enters from the back carrying a cross. Mary remains unaware of the cross even as it enters the chancel and takes up a place in front of the communion table. A tableau is formed by the end of the music with Mary kneeling in front of the cross with baby Jesus cradled in her arms. The figures remain in this position through the communion meditation. They may exit at the beginning of the communion hymn.

Meditation:
Today as we come to the table, the bread and the wine remind us of the great, the powerful love of God. Here is no simplistic, shallow, sentimental love, but one so strong it faces death to be born as flesh and dwell among us. In this feast we find hope in a love so full, it would be poured out in forgiveness for all the world. "As often as you eat this bread and drink the cup, you proclaim the Lord's death until he comes" (1 Corinthians 11:26). Rich meaning is found in this mingling of birth and death: Christmas and the cross. Let us come to the table with ever-increasing thanksgiving to celebrate the presence of our Lord Jesus Christ, born as the Child of Bethlehem; born to live, born to die, born to save poor ordinary people like you and I.

Prayer for the Bread:
God of hope, we come to this feast with hearts thankful for the gift of your Son, born as flesh to dwell among us. As we share this bread together, may it be to us the bread of life, empowering us as individual disciples and as the church to be the body of Christ in and for the life of the world. Amen.

Prayer for the Cup:
God of Christ, we celebrate the birth of your Son with joy. Yet this cup is filled with his life poured out on the cross. This cup is filled with his love, offered for the forgiveness of sins. May these small, symbolic sips so fill our hearts that the love of Jesus Christ might overflow into all the world, through ministries of forgiveness and hope in his name. Amen.

(LOS)

Christmastide/Epiphany

Growing in the Power of
God's Presence

Three days after we put up the Christmas tree, one strand of lights went out. So much for magical moments. Suddenly this tree that had sparkled with the perfect hope of the Advent season was flawed. Because of the peculiar way the lights were strung, it was almost impossible to take them off without undecorating the whole tree. That was just too much work.

I tried to look at the "bright" side. Not all the lights were out, and if you sat at one end of the couch you hardly noticed any difference. My husband was not convinced. He could not stand to look at the tree. Its less than perfect presence perturbed him to no end. He pointed out the flaw to everyone who visited our house. They in turn would politely murmur their condolences, all the while wondering what all the fuss was about.

What was all the fuss about, anyway? We live in a less than perfect world. Amid all the problems that we face each day, a semi-lighted Christmas tree hardly seems tragic. Yet it sums up the feel of Christmastide. The beauty of Christmas Eve with its proclamations of "goodwill to all" and the Epiphany theme of announcement of the gospel to the Gentiles is followed by the realization that even Jesus had to be smuggled out of his homeland to avoid the slaughter of innocent children. His childhood is one of growing in wisdom and stature, which is confirmed at his baptism with the blessing, "This is my Son, the Beloved, with whom I am well pleased." But this beloved son is experienced as a "semi-lighted" presence. He bickers with his mother at Cana and his first sermon perturbs the hometown congregation. We hear again the words from Micah, Jonah, Jeremiah, and Isaiah along with Jesus' proclamation, "No prophet is accepted in the prophet's hometown." It's just too much work.

Christmastide is the season of making sense of God's presence in the world from the wonder of the incarnation to the fleshing out of this presence in the teachings and actions of God in Jesus Christ. Celebrating communion during Christmastide and Epiphany is a shimmer of light in the darkness of midwinter. No more, no less.

1. Meditation and Prayer

"Silent night, holy night, all is calm"—goes the carol. That's not the way it reads in my Bible. First there were the crowds of people coming in for the census—so many that all the hotels were full. One poor, stressed hotel keeper had filled all the beds in the house and still they kept knocking on his door. People were sleeping everywhere. Why, he even bedded an expecting couple out in the barn. Then there were shepherds working night shift who were disturbed by a flock of heavenly hosts who said, "Go; hurry!" There were astrologers from afar who had to pack to travel and figure out what gifts to take with them for Christmas. Then, of course, there was that whole political uproar making the news in Jerusalem. All is calm? I don't think so.

Except maybe at the manger—in his presence. Maybe here in the midst of Christmas chaos we can be in his presence and calm our hearts and feel the radiant beams from his holy face and know the dawn of redeeming grace.

(CDN)

Prayer:

God, we come before you in our strength and wealth, not knowing in our hearts that our strength is really weakness and that our wealth is really poverty. It is so very difficult for us to comprehend that those things that we see as strong are really weak. It is almost beyond our ability to understand that in the weakness of pain and suffering and death there is a strength and power beyond our imagination. We present ourselves to you, the God who became human, the God who became a helpless baby in the poverty of a manger, the God who died in weakness and suffering. Forgive our misplaced trust in the power and wealth of this world and open our blind eyes in this bread and wine to recognize the Lord in the suffering servant, to know the Leader in the small child, and to recognize the greatest in the Kingdom among those who are the least. Amen.

(KT)

2. Communion Meditation

See the child in yonder manger,
So strong and yet so small.
Friend of friends, he'll know no stranger,
As he grows both straight and tall.
Baby boy, God's endless wonder,
Sent to give his loving call.
In this crude and simple manger
Lies the answer to it all.

From the gurglings of the cradle,
To the wailings of the cross,
Body broken for my failures,
For my sins, his life was lost.
In the symbols of his passion,
I receive God's grace anew.
Life restored, my heart rekindled,
Bread and wine, my life renewed.

I will use my hands to serve him,
I will find new ways to care,
All the love this baby gives me,
I will always want to share.
May each child who longs to know him,
In this place and everywhere,
Come to know this child, this Savior,
Through the sacrifice he dared.

(KEW)

3. Meditation and Prayer

A story from the Talmud tells of a king whose son became bitterly angry and left home. Searching him out, the king sent a message asking the son to come home. "I cannot return," came the bitter reply. The king then sent another message, "Return as far as you can, and I will come to you the rest of the way."

The message of Christmas is the message of a God who came to us. In a dirty, dark stable, God came to us in the form of a small child. And it was that child who enabled us to return to God.

As we come to the table this day, may we come with the trust of a child, knowing that it is here that we will find God waiting for us. In the bread, and in the cup, may we remember again the sacrifice of that little child upon the cross, and of the gracious and loving God who could not, would not, let us go.

Prayer:

Most gracious and heavenly God, you have loved us more completely than any earthly love we could know. Like a mother with her child, you have continually sought us out when we would turn away from you. You have followed us when, in our rebellion, we have run away. You have offered us your forgiveness as often as we would repent and turn again to you.

In this communion service, you provide a means of receiving your grace. In the gifts of bread and cup you call to mind the sacrifice of your Son, his body and blood upon the cross. As we partake of these gifts, may they call to mind not only the sacrifice, but the salvation; not only our own sins, but your overwhelming grace.

May your Spirit consecrate the elements that they may be for us the body and blood of Christ; that we may become the body of Christ redeemed by his blood. And may they fill us with such a renewed sense of grace that when we leave this table we will go forth ready to serve and bear witness to you. We ask these things in the name of our Lord Jesus Christ. Amen.

(SM)

4. A Prayer for the Bread

Tender God,
As we gather around this table
in the Christmas season,
We remember that,
before there was a table,
there was a manger
and a mother.

God of all songs!
What lullabies did she sing her little one?
She whom we remember
with our "Silent Night,"
our "Away in a Manger."

We, who now gather as angels, singing,
"Gloria! In Excelsis Deo!"
As shepherds, singing,
"Joy to the World!"

And remembering the wisest of the wise,
Who knew this king would not rule
as an ordinary king,
whose gift was the myrrh of burial.

And now, O God,
because you have given us a table
as well as a manger,
We remember all your children,
loved and unloved;
As we eat the bread of heaven,
we remember all who struggle for food.

And we, with more than our share
of the world's goods,
remember the myrrh that binds us
to a suffering world.

Let your Spirit,
a Spirit of memory,
fill us with good things!

(CC)

5. Litany for Communion
(Luke 2:8–20)

Elder: "An angel of God stood before them,
and the glory of the Lord shone around them."

Minister: Here in the breaking of bread and the sharing of a
cup, we celebrate God's presence and the glory of
God shines around us.

People: FOR ALL WE HAVE HEARD, FOR ALL WE HAVE SEEN,
GLORY BE TO GOD IN THE HIGHEST!

Elder: "Be not afraid; for see—I am bringing you good
news of great joy for all the people."

Minister: Here, in the feast of joy, broken lives are made
whole. Those who are separated are gathered together. Good news for all the people!

People: FOR ALL WE HAVE HEARD, FOR ALL WE HAVE SEEN,
GLORY BE TO GOD IN THE HIGHEST!

Elder: "To you is born this day in the city of David a
Savior, who is the Messiah, the Lord!"

Minister: Here, on this day, Christ comes to you: born in the
saving love of God; present in the sharing of bread
and wine.

All: FOR ALL WE HAVE HEARD, FOR ALL WE HAVE SEEN,
GLORY BE TO GOD IN THE HIGHEST!

(JF)

6. Communion Liturgy

Offertory Prayer:

Gracious God, we approach this table
with the offering of our hearts
and the work of our hands.
With deep thanksgiving for life,
we give from the bounty we have been given.
We can neither pretend to deserve such abundance
any more than your many children without,
nor ignore the responsibility it brings
to help those who are deprived,
for whatever reason.

With humility in your presence,
we bring bread and wine for your blessing.
Through Jesus Christ,
whose name and ministry we choose to bear. Amen.

Litany of Remembrance:

Leader: At this table we are invited to remember....

People: WE REMEMBER WHY WE HAVE COME—WE HAVE COME AT THE INVITATION OF OUR LORD JESUS CHRIST.

Leader: In this company of disciples, we are invited to remember....

People: WE REMEMBER HOW JESUS ATE WITH FRIENDS WHO WOULD DENY HIM AND WITH "SINNERS" WHO BELIEVED HIM.

Leader: In the presence of the empty cross, we are invited to remember....

People: WE REMEMBER THE STORY OF SACRIFICE AND RESURRECTION OF THE LAMB OF GOD WHO TAKES AWAY THE SIN OF THE WORLD.

Communion Prayer:

God, in our Lord and Savior
we have seen your love made visible
in acts of justice and mercy.
We have heard your word clearly
in the message of his life.
We have tasted the goodness of salvation
in his death on our behalf.
With thankful praise we now eat this bread
and remember his broken body.
We drink this cup of covenant
and remember in whom we live and move
and have our being. Amen.

Post-communion Prayer:

God of this feast, by your grace our souls have been fed:
The bread of life nourishes our growth as your children.
The cup of blessing quenches our thirst for living water.
We leave the family table with the power of your presence,
    our guide and strength.
In the name of him who feasts with you forever. Amen.

(MAP)

7. Litany for Communion

[Incorporating "Break the Bread of Belonging" by Brian Wren, text © 1984 by Hope Publishing Co., Carol Stream IL 60188. All rights reserved. Used by permission.]

Worship Setting: Hang posters near communion table with pictures of refugees and other wanderers.

Cantor (sung): Break the bread of belonging,
Welcome the stranger in the land.
We have each been a stranger,
We can try to understand.

People (sung): BREAK THE BREAD OF BELONGING,
WELCOME THE STRANGER IN THE LAND.
WE HAVE EACH BEEN A STRANGER,
WE CAN TRY TO UNDERSTAND.

Reader 1: You shall not oppress a hired servant who is poor and needy, whether she is one of your kindred or one of the sojourners who are in your land within your towns;

Reader 2: You shall give them their hire on the day they earn it, before the sun goes down (Deuteronomy 24:14–15a, adapted).

Elder: The ministry of hospitality is ours. Let us prepare a welcoming table for all of Christ's people.

People: BUT WHO ARE THEY? HOW WILL WE KNOW THEM?

Choir (sung): Traveling, traveling, over the world,
people can be out of place,
dashing for freedom, looking for work,
needing a friendly face.

People (sung): BREAK THE BREAD OF BELONGING,
WELCOME THE STRANGER IN THE LAND.
WE HAVE EACH BEEN A STRANGER,
WE CAN TRY TO UNDERSTAND.

Cantor (sung): Break the bread of belonging,
Fear of the foreigner still blows strong;
Make a space for the strangers,
Give them the right to belong.

Reader 1: The right to belong? But who are these people? Where do they come from? They may crowd us out. They make too many demands on us....

Reader 2: What are the troubles that bring them to us? What are they hoping to find?

Both readers: And just who gave them the right to belong?

Choir (sung): Some have fled from terror by night,
hiding from bullets by day,
weary and hungry, in fear of their life,
seeking a safe place to stay.

Reader 1: Now when the visitors from the East departed, behold, an angel of the Lord appeared to Joseph in a dream and said, "Rise, take the child and his mother, and flee to Egypt, and remain there till I tell you; for Herod is about to search for the child, to destroy him." And he rose and took the child and his mother by night, and departed to Egypt (Matthew 2:13–14).

Elder: Refugees, with a tiny child—Mary, Joseph, and Jesus. We have read Matthew so many times that we may not notice this. The holy family, fugitives in Egypt, fleeing political turmoil, certain death for their newborn son...strangers needing shelter, needing to belong...and then ask us: "Is *this* a safe place? Do we belong?"

Cantor and People (sung): BREAK THE BREAD OF BELONGING,
WELCOME THE STRANGER IN THE LAND.
WE HAVE EACH BEEN A STRANGER,
WE CAN TRY TO UNDERSTAND.

BREAK THE BREAD OF BELONGING,
FEAR OF THE FOREIGNER STILL BLOWS STRONG;
MAKE A SPACE FOR THE STRANGERS,
GIVE THEM THE RIGHT TO BELONG.

Choir (sung): Some are far from the people they love,
driven by family need,
tired and exploited, doing their job,
thinking of children to feed.

Elder: It is not enough to spread the table and invite all those who believe to come. The ministry of hospitality drives us out into an inhospitable world, to change economic policies and systems that cut off families from one another, that force people to work in inhumane conditions, or force them not to work because of the lack of proper child care. Breaking the bread of belonging is not a one-day-a-week proposition. Breaking the bread of belonging is the way of life to which God calls us.

Reader 2: When you reap the harvest in your field, and have forgotten a sheaf in the field, you shall not go back to go get it; it shall be for the sojourner, the orphan, and the widow; that the Lord your God may bless you in all the work of your hands. When you beat your olive trees, you shall not go over the boughs again; it shall be for the sojourner, the orphan, and the widow. When you gather the grapes of your vineyard, you shall not glean it afterward (Deuteronomy 24:19–21).

Choir: Traveling, traveling, over the world,
No one should be out of place.
What would we say, then, if we were alone,
needing a friendly face?

All (sung): BREAK THE BREAD OF BELONGING,
WELCOME THE STRANGER IN THE LAND.
WE HAVE EACH BEEN A STRANGER,
WE CAN TRY TO UNDERSTAND.

BREAK THE BREAD OF BELONGING,
FEAR OF THE FOREIGNER STILL BLOWS STRONG;
MAKE A SPACE FOR THE STRANGERS,
GIVE THEM THE RIGHT TO BELONG.

Unison prayer: GUARDIAN OF THE OPPRESSED, THE HOMELESS, ALL THOSE WHO WANDER, WATCH OVER YOUR CHILDREN THIS DAY. PREPARE OUR HEARTS AS WE SHARE THIS MEAL THAT WE MIGHT BECOME THE BREAD OF LIFE TO THOSE WHO HAVE NO HOPE. FIRE WITHIN US A PASSION FOR JUSTICE AND HOSPITALITY, THAT YOUR WANDERING CHILDREN WILL TRULY FIND THEMSELVES AT HOME WITH US AND WITH YOU. AMEN.

(OIH)

8. Meditation and Prayers
(Luke 2:22–40)

One day, quite unexpectedly, a young woman discovered she had found undeserved favor with God. God's action, not Mary's, had led her to receive unmerited favor. However, though the angelic messenger of grace said she would be called "blessed," within a year a wise old man named Simeon prophesied a sword would pierce her soul as well (Luke 2:35). Surely Mary must have wondered at such a mixed message. Grace leads to blessing and suffering? How can this be? But, puzzled or not, she responded by saying "yes" to God.

As people of faith we have also said "yes" to God. Our baptismal covenant with God said we believe in and accept the undeserved favor we receive from God. We say "yes" to God's ever-flowing love which washes over us and makes us clean. The communion cup and bread are reminders of God's blessing of grace.

However, at least by the world's standards, we too receive a mixed message. With the blessing of grace there are no promises of life without pain or trial. Further, by responding to God's grace, by loving as Jesus loved, we may even increase our suffering. When we partake of the cup and the broken bread we declare we are willing to carry the burdens of others. So with Mary we may discover that saying "yes" to God brings blessing as well as potential suffering.

This communion table reminds us of the undeserved favor we find through Jesus. We are indeed blessed. Let us renew our baptismal vows, and join Mary to say "yes" to God. May we leave this table empowered to love as we are loved.

Prayer for the Bread:

God of Grace, we remember Jesus said "yes" to you by living and dying in the name of love. This broken bread reminds us that love is willing to pay a price. With this bread, nourish us with courage to follow in his example. Because of Jesus' broken body, we pray. Amen.

Prayer for the Cup:

God of Justice, we know that injustice rules when the innocent or powerless in your creation suffer. We confess that we contribute to suffering when we love too little. Forgive us and empower us to drink from the same cup of Jesus that we too may live and die in the name of love. Because of Jesus' love, we pray. Amen. (BD)

9. Litany for Communion
(John 1:14–16)

One: "And the Word became flesh and dwelt among us, full of grace and truth" (John 1:14a, RSV).

Many: BUT WE WERE AFRAID OF THE FLESH, O GOD: SO HUMAN AND FILLED WITH PASSIONS AND NEEDS; SO DARING TO TOUCH AND TO EMBRACE THE HUMANITY OF ANOTHER.

One: "And the Word became flesh and dwelt among us, full of grace and truth."

Many: BUT WE WERE AFRAID OF DWELLING TOO CLOSE TO THE FLESH, GOD. THE HUMAN ONE MIGHT NEED CLEANSING, MIGHT DEMAND OUR CARE. THE CHILD MIGHT BE HUNGRY, MIGHT ASK FOR OUR FOOD.

One: "And the Word became flesh and dwelt among us, full of grace and truth."

Many: BUT WE WERE AFRAID OF THE TRUTH, O GOD. AFRAID OF ONE WHO CAME TO TELL US ABOUT OURSELVES. THE WORD IS NO LONGER DISTANT, BUT IS BORN A CHILD IN OUR MIDST.

One: "And the Word became flesh and dwelt among us, full of grace and truth."

Many: AND WE WERE AFRAID OF THE GRACE, O GOD; FOR SURELY YOU COULD NOT FORGIVE THE BROKENNESS AND FAILURES OF OUR HUMAN LIVES.

One: The Word became flesh and dwelt among us that we may have new life in God's grace. In the sharing of bread and wine we receive that human flesh broken and life-blood given.

Many: AT THE TABLE OF THE CHRIST, WE EMBRACE OUR HUMANITY, DARE TO DWELL WITH OUR BROTHERS AND SISTERS, ACCEPT THE TRUTH, AND TRUST IN GOD'S GRACE.

All: "WE HAVE BEHELD THE WORD'S GLORY, GLORY AS OF THE ONLY CHILD FROM GOD....AND FROM THE FULLNESS OF THE CHILD HAVE WE ALL RECEIVED, GRACE UPON GRACE" (John 1:14b, 16, adapted).

(JF)

10. Communion Confession
(Matthew 5:1–12)

"Blessed are those who hunger and thirst for righteousness, for they will be filled" (verse 6).

The table spread before us reminds us of how the world is hungering and thirsting. Humanity hungers and thirsts for power, for domination, for the accumulation of material goods. The world hungers to "do to the others before they do it to you." This hunger results in cruelty and dehumanization and domination of the weakest. The world's hunger is turned into itself and devours all in its path. Crucifixion.

The world is hungry and God walked among us and we knew it not.

Spilled blood and broken bodies.

But the people of faith hunger and thirst for righteousness to prevail, hunger for justice in this unjust world, hunger for the experience of belonging, and hunger for welcoming open arms for all. We hunger to make into a reality Jesus' healing vision of love and justice. God walks among us today, making us hungry for spiritual fulfillment.

The bread and cup remind us of these two kinds of hunger: the world's destructive cravings that persecute and crucify and the faithful people's hunger for righteousness to prevail.

We come to this table aware that the vision is not yet fulfilled, perhaps because we aren't hungry enough for it.

Jesus invites us. Come to this table hungry for righteousness. Come to this table hungry for God's presence. And you shall be filled.

Prayer of Confession:
God of justice and compassion, forgive us for being satiated. Forgive us when we have failed to see your vision, when we have not hungered or thirsted for righteousness. When we live by our own standards we cannot tell the difference between your righteousness and our own self-righteousness. Fill us with the desire for righteous living, the courage to make the changes, to take the stands, to live steadfastly and to remain faithful. Renew us with the bread of life. In the name of Jesus, our example of righteousness, Amen.

(BD)

11. For Epiphany Sunday
(1 Corinthians 8:1–13)

In a recent novel, there is a family that cannot, simply cannot, eat a meal together.* Every time they sit down for dinner, they hurl sharp words back and forth. The verbal warfare always continues until some family member runs from the table in anger. Year after year, the painful pattern repeats and every meal ends in tight-lipped anger and an empty chair. Instead of times of sharing, mealtimes become a ritual of anger.

The children grow and leave home. One brother opens a restaurant that he calls the Homesick Restaurant. He wants to create a place where everyone feels welcome. He wants to create a feeling of togetherness that he missed growing up.

Years later, the children return to the town for a day. The whole starched and pressed gang troops over to the Homesick Restaurant for dinner. As they sip their ice water and scan the menus, the inevitable squabbling begins. Their voices grow shrill, faces redden, and neck muscles begin to bulge with tension. Suddenly, a chair is knocked over, and one member races away from the table and out the door.

In the silence, the restaurant-owning brother speaks softly. "For once, I want this family to finish a meal together. We cannot afford any more empty chairs." Searching, they find the outcast and bring him back. They sit down at the table— an ordinary family with the ordinary fights. And they finish the meal...together.

This table is prepared in love. The gift of Christ is a sign that although we are all sinners, we are welcome at the feast. Put aside whatever holds you back, and join your brothers and sisters in a new way of living.

Prayer:

God, we sit here today with the same old problems. Brothers and sisters at the same table, we quarrel like children over who's right and who's wrong. We gather our arguments, take sides, shout out proofs and statistics. In our drive to be bigger and better than, we have forgotten that the victory is in surrender.

Forgive us, Lord; we have tried to outshout each other and justify ourselves. We have cared more about being right than being righteous. We have looked around the table for opponents, never seeing brothers and sisters.

We are humbled in your house, Lord. Here at your table, we remember that there are no favorites. We remember that we have all blundered; not one of us is perfect. And yet, you continue to serve us with grace. You offer forgiveness and help us forgive each other. In your presence, healing begins.

Open our eyes to a new age vision, Lord. Help us look deep inside this meal of ordinary bread and juice to see an extraordinary sight. Let us eat abundantly of new world hope, let us drink deeply of the expectation that in you, the world can be transformed. Help us to see a global family; give us power to broaden the table; help us take your bread and wine into all the world, arms full of the bread of forgiveness, clutching jugs that brim with new life.

In the name of Jesus Christ, who is the bread of salvation and the cup of redemption, refresh our spirits, and create us anew. Amen.

(LSM)

* Anne Tyler, *Dinner at the Homesick Restaurant.*

12. For Epiphany Sunday

So often we come to the table trying to achieve an inward, personal, spiritual peace. We want to sit quietly, eyes closed, meditating and reflecting on the word of God as it may speak secretly to our hearts and our needs. We come wanting to leave it all behind, to forget the troubles and tribulations lurking just outside the sanctuary doors.

Yet just when we think we're getting there—suddenly a blaring, screeching fire engine or ambulance races by. Sirens scream in our ears, tearing at our hearts, reminding us of the pain, violence, and fear all around us and within. Or maybe it is the reverberating sound system of a passing car pounding so loudly that it rocks the windows in the sanctuary. We feel irritated with a world that is too mundane, too secular.

Sometimes the source of disturbance of our personal, inward peace is found within the walls of the sanctuary as that new baby two rows back starts wailing, or the elderly man with Alzheimer's begins murmuring loudly, out of turn.

Out of aggravation, we start wishing for a nice, quiet place where only the songs of birds would edify our contemplations.

How nice everything would be if we could only silence those irritants. Surely, in the pristine silence of the sanctuary we could properly focus on the meaning of this broken bread and wine without distraction.

"In Christ God was reconciling the world..." (2 Corinthians 5:19a).

Contrary to how we might want to read this text, God here is not going about the business of obliterating the differences between sacred and secular. Rather, in Christ, God and the world, different as they are, *meet*, and are one through the at-one-ment. God and the world were gathered "In Christ," not for *conformity*, but for *community*. In Christ, God and the world are one. So the church is challenged to open the sanctuary doors wide, to let the world in, and indeed to go out offering the reconciliation of God in Christ, which embraces differences in a gathering of love, respect, and forgiveness. We are called to bring the table out of the ivory tower of piety and to sit down with the whole world to feast on God's love through bread and wine.

(DOS/LOS)

Prayer:

Our Dear Jesus, be to us as you were to the wise men. Show us your star that we may know your presence in our world. May we have the faith to see your star. May we have the vision to know where it guides us. May we have the courage to follow where it leads. Like the wise men we have our own horded treasures. As we find you, may we have the wisdom to open our treasure chests, to rid ourselves of our unholy dependence on the things of this world. May we give up our old ways of living. May we forsake the old paths that we have trod and turn and follow a new road. As we find you may the old pass away and the new come that your star may signify your new creation in our souls. Amen.

(KT)

13. Prayer for the Bread
(Winter)

Deep calls to deep!
In this winter season,
when the resting earth
offers no green leaf or bright flower
to evoke our easy joy,
We turn to our deeper places
to learn thanksgiving.
We learn the thanks of waiting,
of hope,
of the faith that dwells amid uncertainties.

And we contemplate the miracle of bread,
appearing before us on this table,
when the earth gives no sign
of last year's wheat,
or next's.

So, with no warning,
but with mighty grace, O God,
did you, hearing the cries of enslaved Israel,
free them
and plant them
in a land flowing with milk and honey.

And so did you send Jesus the Christ
to a world in pain,
Who, feeding us with the bread of the earth,
taught us the meaning
of abundant love.

Send now your Spirit, God,
that we may know the miracle of silent earth,
the miracle of bread,
the miracle of our love for each other,
reflecting your love for us.

And send us, thus empowered,
to respond to a world
where winter daunts
both bread and love.

(CC)

14. Prayers for Bread and Cup

Prayer for the Bread:

O God, we are like your prophet Jonah. Like Jonah we hear your word but we arise and flee from your presence. We flee from you and cut ourselves off from you. We alienate ourselves from you and like Jonah we are cast into the sea. We are in the midst of the deep, far from your presence. The waters close in around us and chaos sweeps us away. Of our rebellion against you we repent. O Lord, as you did for Jonah so also do for us. Appoint for us a great fish to swallow us up into your abundant mercy and grace. Appoint for us a great fish to deliver us from the sea of our rebellion. Appoint for us a great fish to carry us out of our chaos to the safety and order of your dry ground. Dear God, appoint for us a great fish to save us.

In this bread of life make us aware that our prayer is answered, that we have been rescued from our sea of chaos and sin. In this bread of life make us know that you have sent to us your great fish of salvation. In this bread of life may we know Jesus Christ, Son of God, our Savior. Amen.

(KT)

(Isaiah 61; Luke 4:18)

Prayer for the Cup:

Loving God,
We give thanks for this cup,
which is a symbol of your steadfast love,
poured out for us in the blood of Jesus.
We give thanks that in this cup each of us
can find forgiveness, new hope, and new beginnings.
But God, we confess that too often we forget
that "for us" does not mean "just for me."
We forget that
if good news is to be proclaimed to the poor
and liberty to the captive,
it must be proclaimed with our voices.
We forget that
if the blind are to see
and the oppressed to be set free,
our hearts and our hands must be
open to your spirit and
dedicated to your service.

Forgive us, O Lord.
Renew us and strengthen us.
Help us to make our living
a reflection of your love.
In Jesus' name, Amen.

(CE)

15. Responsive Prayer

Elder: Blessed are you, O God, ruler of the universe.
It is you who creates us as your people
and brings us to this place
to celebrate this feast with thanksgiving.

People: YOU HAVE KINDLED THE LIGHTS OF CREATION.
WE SEE YOU IN THE LIGHT
AND SENSE YOUR WARMTH AND LOVE.
YOU BRING FORTH THE FRUIT FROM THE VINE
AND BREAD FROM THE EARTH.
WE TASTE AND KNOW THAT YOU ARE GOOD.
WE ARE DRAWN TO THE FRAGRANCE OF YOUR PRESENCE.

Elder: Send your Spirit now upon these gifts that Jesus'
own words may be fulfilled:
"My body, broken for you."
"My blood of the covenant, poured out for you."

People: AS WE RECEIVE THESE ELEMENTS,
MAY CHRIST BE BROUGHT INTO OUR REMEMBRANCE;
MAY WE SEE THE POSSIBILITIES IN CREATION;
AND MAY WE BE NOURISHED AND EMPOWERED
FOR SERVANTHOOD IN YOUR WORLD.

(LPR)

Lent

Struggling with the Reality
of a Present Power

A friend once told me that she admires the beauty of trees in the dead of winter. Stripped of leaves, their individuality stands out. Each is distinctive in the twist of its branches and the shades of gray that color its bark. I much prefer the beauty of fall when the landscape is aflame with brilliant colors and a mere glance out the window can brighten my day. Appreciating the beauty of barren trees is an acquired taste that requires an eye trained to see shades of gray.

Lent is a gray season. It begins with the grayness of ash, which signals our need to look at the grayness of our own lives and the memory of Jesus' own struggle with temptation. It continues with a perplexing chorus of God's presence in history. The promise of covenants, the miracles of Jesus, and the triumphal entry into Jerusalem stand alongside the sacrifice of Isaac, the valley of dry bones, and the cross. At the heart of this season is Maundy Thursday, which receives its name not from the institution of the Lord's Supper but from Jesus' command to "love one another...as I have loved you" (John 13:34), which is symbolized by washing the feet of the disciples.

We may come to admire the mystery of this grayness of life lived in the present power of God. Still, it's hard to give up a secret longing for a presence that would instantly brighten our days. The challenge of communion during Lent is not to give in to this desire for easy answers. Lent is the season of coming to terms with the magnitude and mystery of God's present power in the life of Israel, of Jesus, and in our own lives. In doing so we see the beauty of God's presence within the branches of our lives.

1. Litany for Communion

Elder 1: "If we say that we have no sin, we deceive ourselves, and the truth is not in us" (1 John 1:8).

Elder 2: "If we confess our sins, [God] who is faithful and just will forgive us and cleanse us from all unrighteousness" (1 John 1:9).

Elder 1: Paul calls us to examine ourselves, and "only then to eat of the bread and drink of the cup" (1 Corinthians 11:28).

Elder 2: Here, in the presence of God and of one another, let us search our hearts and confess our sins to the God who is near at hand.

(Silence)

Elder 1: O God, as your Spirit drove Jesus into the desert (Mark 1:12), we are driven by our desire for you to this table.

People: OUR SOULS THIRST FOR YOU, O GOD. OUR BODIES LONG FOR YOU LIKE A DESERT (Psalm 63:1).

Elder 2: We know that we have strayed from your path of mercy and justice, both as individuals and as a community. We pray to be forgiven and transformed.

People: OUR SOULS THIRST FOR YOU, O GOD. OUR BODIES LONG FOR YOU LIKE A DESERT.

Elder 1:   We remember those we have wronged, and the things
we have done that have divided us from you.
We long to be reunited with our sisters and brothers.
We long to be reunited with you.

People: OUR SOULS THIRST FOR YOU, O GOD.
OUR BODIES LONG FOR YOU LIKE A DESERT.

Elder 2:   And so at your gracious invitation,
we join one another to meet you at this table,
where faithful people have sought you age after age.

People: OUR SOULS THIRST FOR YOU, O GOD.
OUR BODIES LONG FOR YOU LIKE A DESERT.

Elder 1:   Creating God, we give you thanks for the gift of
bread, formed by hands of tender strength.
As we share this bread of life,
illuminate the invisible bonds that unite us to one
another, to you, and to faithful people everywhere.

People: OUR SOULS THIRST FOR YOU, O GOD.
OUR BODIES LONG FOR YOU LIKE A DESERT.

Elder 2:   Creating God, we give you thanks for this cup,
gift of your fruitful earth.
As we share this cup of hope,
draw us ever nearer to one another and to you.

People: OUR SOULS THIRST FOR YOU, O GOD.
OUR BODIES LONG FOR YOU LIKE A DESERT.

Words of Institution

Sharing of the Bread and Cup

Unison: O GOD WHO CALLED US INTO LIFE,
AS WE PASS YOUR GIFTS FROM HAND TO HAND,
WE REMEMBER THAT YOU CALLED US
TO LIVE AS DIVINE CREATIONS,
BEARING THE POSSIBILITIES OF LIFE AND HOPE AND LOVE.
WE PRAY THAT WE MAY NEVER CEASE TO STRUGGLE
TO PERCEIVE YOUR PROMISE IN OURSELVES AND OTHERS.
STRENGTHENED BY YOUR GIFTS,
WE GO FORTH AS YOUR PEOPLE,
EVER LONGING FOR YOUR PRESENCE
AND EAGER TO RESPOND TO YOUR CALL TO US. AMEN!

(SP)

2. Prayer

Eternal and most loving God, we come to this your table with praise and thanksgiving, because it is here that we experience most profoundly the breadth and depth of your love for us. It was in the upper room that your Son revealed to his disciples the meaning of sacrificial love in the washing of feet, the breaking of bread, and the sharing of the cup. It was there that sin ruptured the very sacredness of that moment in the complicity and betrayal of a disciple. It was there that humility as a mark of true discipleship was revealed by Jesus as the disciples disputed among themselves which of them was the greatest.

We thank you, God, for your constant presence in our lives, for your reaching out to us, showing us your will and giving us strength and courage to do as you would have us do. We thank you for the life, death and resurrection of your Son, Jesus Christ, and the assurance of newness of life.

Forgive us, God, when we have not been faithful servants. Forgive us when we have turned aside from the suffering of persons close at hand and far away. Forgive us when we have been guided by the voices of the world and have turned deaf ears to your voice as you speak to us in the depths of our conscience.

As we partake of this bread and this cup, create within us pure hearts, that we may hear your voice. Open our eyes to the needs of the weak, the hungry, the sick, the dispossessed, the imprisoned, that with compassion we may live out the role of servants. Send us forth with renewed hope and faith. In the name of Jesus we pray. Amen.

(VL, from *The Gifts We Bring*, Vol. 2)

3. Meditation and Prayer

Can you imagine the communion table without a cross? (*Remove the cross from the table and set it out of view.*) Can you imagine the life of Jesus without a cross?

The cross is so essential to what we do at this table. The cross is so essential to what we do when we remember who

Jesus is as the Christ. And yet how often do we go through our lives as if there is no cross? How often do we separate ourselves from that sacrifice, that dedication, of doing what God calls us to do?

Oh, we talk about our cross sometimes, about taking up our cross and following Christ, but so often what we talk about is not what his cross is all about. When Jesus said, "Take up [your] cross and follow me" (Mark 8:34), he wasn't talking about life's burdens that are thrust upon us, things we do simply because we have to do them, difficult things we must bear, or trials we must go through.

Rather, he was talking about the cross of total obedience to God. He was talking about doing what God calls you to do as a child of God. He was talking about putting God first, giving yourself regardless of what sacrifice it might call from you. (*Replace the cross during next words.*)

The cross is central to this table, for here we come to see ourselves in relation to Jesus Christ. We come to hear his call to take up our cross and follow him.

(DC)

Prayer:
Eternal God, we come to this your table aware of your constant and faithful presence with us in our waking and in our sleeping, in our work and in our play, in our joy and in our sorrows, and in every relationship. We are aware that you are present here in a very real sense, speaking to us of love and sacrifice and ultimate meaning.

As we partake of this bread and this cup, symbols of Christ's broken body, speak to us of broken bodies in our world today that cry out for the healing power of your Spirit. As we remember the invincible spirit of your Son on the cross, speak to us of the agony of minds and hearts around us, tormented by fear, paralyzed by hate, and isolated by loneliness. As we partake of this bread and this cup, fill us with your Spirit that we may depend upon your healing power and that we may speak of wholeness, of health, of love, and of joy in your name. In the name of Jesus we pray. Amen.

(VL, from *The Gifts We Bring*, Vol. 2)

4. Prayer for the Cup
(Psalm 23)

God is my shepherd,
I shall not want.

God makes me lie down in green pastures,
leads me beside still waters,
restores my life.

In this season of prayer and preparation,
nourishing God,
let this cup be to us
as a pool of still water,
where we contemplate and discover,
under every loss and sorrow,
under every passing joy,
the deep reality
that in you
we do not want.

And from this discovery,
let our cups overflow
with thanksgiving
in every act of goodness and mercy
in the world—
your true home—
our whole lives long.

(CC)

5. Communion Meditation
(Mark 14:18)

As Jesus sat at table with his disciples, he looked at them and said, "Truly I tell you, one of you will betray me" (Mark 14:18). Naturally, the disciples were horrified, and quickly they denied the possibility. Yet, before the night was through, they all betrayed Jesus in some way: by selling him out to the highest bidder, by denying him before others, by abandoning him in his greatest need. And yet, even knowing what was to come, Jesus sat at table with them and shared with them the bread of life and the cup of salvation.

Like the disciples, we too have betrayed Jesus. We have abandoned his teachings in our hunger for money and power.

We have betrayed his self-giving Spirit in our climb to the top of the corporate ladder. We have denied even knowing him in our unwillingness to love our brothers and sisters. In countless ways we have denied and abandoned our Lord. And yet, even knowing our sinful nature, Jesus continues to invite us to his table, to share with him the bread of life and the cup of salvation.

In this season of Lent, as we reflect on the sacrifice of our Lord upon the cross, may we come to the table truly repentant, confessing our sins, with humility and thanksgiving for the gracious invitation we have received. May we rise from the table cleansed and renewed, strengthened to face the temptations of our world, with humility and thanksgiving for the gracious life we have received.

(SM)

6. Responsive Call to Communion, and Prayer

Celebrant: Arms outstretched as on the cross, you call each of us to communion with you this day, O gentle Savior.

People: AS WE COME TO YOUR BOUNTEOUS TABLE ONCE AGAIN, ENFOLD US IN THOSE SAME LOVING ARMS, RECALLING WITH US THE BITTER TASTE AND TEXTURE OF YOUR SACRIFICE FOR THE WORLD'S SAKE.

Celebrant: Fill us full of your power and grace, reminding us, through the familiar symbols of bread and wine, how very much you love us.

Unison: STAND NOW IN OUR MIDST, BLESSED REDEEMER, AS OUR HOST, OUR SAVIOR, OUR BROTHER, AND OUR FRIEND. AMEN.

Celebrant: Eternal Spirit, giver of our memory and guide to our future, gather us as your family to the table of transformation this day. In the poignant symbol of the bread, may we touch your own body, broken for us. Through the clear image of the cup itself, introduce us once again to the sweetness of God's compassion poured out on us through the bitterness of the cross. Bless now this holy feast as our own spirits are restored to wholeness through the lifeblood of Jesus Christ, in whose name we pray. Amen.

(KEW)

7. Meditation and Prayer
(2 Corinthians 5:16–21)

The German theologian Dietrich Bonhoeffer wrote in *The Cost Of Discipleship*, "When Jesus calls us, he bids us come and die." We, the gathered body of Christ, are ones who have responded to that call. Through Christ, we gain strength to die to the fears that keep us from loving. We gain courage to die to the selfishness that keeps us from sharing our gifts. We learn to die to seeking our own success and salvation in disregard for the good of all God's children.

The good news is that God has promised that if we die with Christ, we will also rise with Christ as new creations, to be God's children, worshiping together, caring about one another, discovering what it means to be fully human. Here at the communion table we find bread for the journey into new life and the cup through which we enter into new covenant with Christ. Jesus calls all of us who believe in him; all are welcome at his table.

Prayer:

God of compassion and hope, we come to the table awed by the mystery of a love greater than we can fathom and thankful for these your gifts, symbols of the body and blood of the Christ. We come with dusty feet, dear God, recognizing our imperfections, our failures, eager to lay to rest our fears and our selfishness, eager for the reassurance that we are yours, that this is your world despite our seeming fascination with sin and death.

Join our lives with one another, as Christ in his death and resurrection linked his life to all others, that we may become your church. Send us forth in service, nourished in the sure knowledge of your love and redemption, which through your grace we are a part. We pray in the name of the living Christ. Amen.

(MB)

8. Communion Meditation

Each winter, an anxious, unsettled, inward awareness begins to well up within me. It comes to fullness during this season as I discover the realness and humanity of Christ. As I reacquaint myself with Jesus' pain, his temptations, his betrayal, I find myself wanting to pray for him, that once again he can hold out and win through.

I think God accepts these tense, uncertain, gut-level prayers for Christ. I also think God accepts our tense, uncertain, sometimes unutterable, gut-level prayers for ourselves. For our fear emerges as we recover our own humanity through Christ:

—fear that this year, this time, we will not be able to hold out and win through;

—fear that we will die without ever having really lived or really loved;

—fear that we will be the one to betray—ourselves, Christ— three times or maybe more;

—fear that the resurrection power cannot possibly be something we could enflesh.

As you commune with God today, pray for yourself:

—that you may be able to trust God working in the dark for you;

—that you may be willing to experience the pain of God's presence;

—that you may be freed from the past with appreciation and freed for the future with readiness.

God is in what is happening in you. The love of God is for you.
(CKC, from *The Gifts We Bring*, Vol. 1)

9. Prayer

O God, you brought us forth from your eternal womb to be your own. You would hold us to your breast to sustain us, but we have resisted you and gone our own way. You would feed us with your body, but we have refused. And now like a lost child we faint from hunger and thirst and do not know which way to turn. We cry out for comfort, but will not be comforted. We reach out to be fed, but will not eat. Forgive us our rejection of you for we have sinned. Reach out to us and pull us close to you. Draw us close to feed us with your body and nourish us with your Spirit. Wrap your arms of love and compassion around us and make us feel safe and secure. Enclose us in the warmth of your embrace that our desire shall be satisfied and our longing fulfilled. Amen.

(KT)

10. Litany

(The congregational response may be sung to a tune in common meter [8.6.8.6.], such as Belmont ["Beneath the Forms of Outward Rite"], Crimond ["The Lord's My Shepherd"], or St. Agnes ["Jesus, the Very Thought of Thee"].)

Leader: We are one body whose head is the Lord Jesus Christ. It is he who invites all of us who name him Savior to come to this table.

People: BEFORE YOUR PRESENCE, LORD, WE STAND
To SHARE A COMMON MEAL:
A LOAF, A CUP, A PRAYER OF THANKS,
A LONGING TO BE REAL.

Leader: We are one body whose many members
serve the whole in differing ways.
Some of us have greater gifts of vision;
others, healing hands.

People: BEFORE YOUR FACE WE HUMBLY KNEEL,
OUR SIN IS PRESENT STILL;
IN BUSY-NESS WE MISS YOUR CARE,
IN SELFISHNESS, YOUR WILL.

Leader: We are one body whose life is a gift of God.
What we make of our body is our gift to God.

People: BEFORE YOUR EYES WE SHALL ARISE
AND SING SHALOM'S SWEET SOUND;
WE GLIMPSE THE WAY, AND HAND IN HAND,
STEP FORTH ON HOLY GROUND.

Elder: Loving God, we have confessed our sin and petitioned your gracious forgiveness. We have studied your word and pondered our place in your story. We have sung your praise and prayed for your children. And now at the family table we find ourselves face to face with the grace you offered in Jesus Christ before we knew we needed it.
Unending Power, in our freedom to choose, we come.
In the power you share, we are bold to come.
In the name of Jesus Christ, the beloved Child, we come. Amen.

(MAP)

11. Meditation and Prayer
(Job 28:1)

This table spread before us could be called a table of sorrow. Spilled blood and broken bodies, humanity's cruelty at Golgotha. Crucifixion is still with us today: economic deprivation, personal isolation, genocide, political exploitation, and destructive relationships. We feel this brokenness. We too carry the scars, sometimes caused by our own choices, sometimes caused by circumstances beyond our control. This table holds the cup and broken bread, the reminders of Good Friday, reminders of the "man of sorrows."

Job was another "man of sorrow" who, in the midst of the most severe trials of disease, death, and loss, brought his sorrows to God. However, instead of sympathy, Job received a challenge to focus on the immediate power of God that ultimately exceeded his human struggle. God asked, "Where were you when I was creating the world? Do you know as much as the Creator?"

As we assemble in the midst of the muck of our human lives and we bring our personal issues, God declares a bold challenge to us through the bread and wine. The communion table declares we must look beyond the sin and sorrow to see a spectacular God.

Dare to believe beyond the obvious!

Dare to believe in life beyond death! Joy beyond sorrow!

Dare to believe in resurrection's power! Love triumphs!

To stay at a table of sorrow is to remain at Good Friday. But to receive the life-giving bread and cup is to move to the joy of the Easter morning. Dare we believe it?

Partake of this bread and wine with thanksgiving and joy! The table of sorrows is transformed.

Prayer of Confession:

O God, this life is so complex, so full of ups and downs, hills and deep valleys, so many turns and changes. It is so easy for us to despair, to forget you are our source of life. We forget that when we "live and move and have our being" in you, we can rejoice no matter what the circumstance. Forgive us when we whine and complain and take our eyes off you. As we eat this bread and drink this cup, fill us with hope and joy of an Easter people. Because of Jesus, Amen.

(BD)

12. Communion Meditation

In the warm, sunlit kitchen behind the sanctuary, my mother, a deaconess, and I would clean up communion after worship. My job was to pour all the juice from the little glass communion cups unused by the worshipers into one large glass. And then, all by myself, I got to drink this symbol of Christ's blood. No tiny sip of juice ever quenched my thirst; I wanted a large full glass of the foamy, purple stuff that went down so sweet and left behind indelible stains at the corners of my mouth. I often wondered, in those days, why they did not serve enough of the juice to satisfy people, to really take the edge off a powerful thirst worked up after a couple of hours of Sunday school and worship? Why did they give you just enough to leave an aftertaste in your mouth, to leave you wanting more?

Now, however, I think it is a good thing that only a taste of juice and a bit of bread is served at the Lord's Table. It is better to get up from the table not quite full, vaguely dissatisfied and yearning for something more. For if we were to eat and drink our fill, we might think that this present feast is all there is to our memorial of Christ's sacrifice. Our hunger and thirst satisfied, we might come to believe that this present moment is not only our past, but our future, *ad infinitum, in perpetuum*. We might forget that the Last Supper shared by Jesus and his disciples was not the final supper; we might forget that another supper awaits us in which plenty and more for everyone will be served. The evangelist Matthew, however, does not forget when he tells of Jesus' last meal with his disciples. "I tell you," Matthew recalls Jesus' words, "I will never again drink of this fruit of the vine until that day when I drink it new with you in my Father's kingdom" (Matthew 26:29).

Memories of full glasses of grape juice, of wine poured from pitcher to chalice, of life spilled for the sake of all blend into one another as we participate in the Lord's Supper. They leave us yearning for more than these few sips and crumbs. Yet these tiny tastes of bread and wine draw us into our future toward the One who in anticipation of sharing with us the feast of plenty and more has already sliced the bread and poured the juice. Then, and only then, will our present foretaste of loaf and cup explode into feasts of enough—enough bread, enough juice to satisfy any hunger or thirst.   (NCP)

13. Prayer for the Cup

God of new birth,
We know—
and often forget—
that the dark stillness of this cup
comes only after
the pouring out
of unshapable liquid.

We know—
and often forget—
that the pouring out
of Jesus' life
did not begin on the cross,
but in his living
the human life:
In his proclamation
that the last be first;
In the flow of his Spirit
to the hemorrhaging woman.

We know—
and often forget—
that our new life
in the Spirit
only begins
when our lips
touch this cup.

Birth anew each moment:
Alive to this world's pain
and empowered to respond,
We sing our song of
transformation
and thanksgiving.

(CC)

14. Meditation and Prayer
(John 12:27–36)

We live in a world fraught with distance. Those moments when we experience intimacy with others are only momentary, and serve to remind us that separation, rather than unity, governs our lives. Indeed, distance defines who we are, and some distances, no doubt we all would agree, are better than others. We keep our distance from those we do not know. We follow each other in our cars on the roads at a safe distance. To look at something carefully, or even to see it at all, we place it at the right distance. We try to imagine the distances that even light only slowly traverses in space, and we wonder at the seemingly infinite distances hidden within the smallest atom. We go to church to cross the distance that ordinarily separates us from God, and yet we still often feel that God is too distant.

The scripture reading today portrays an anxious crowd, surrounding Jesus in hope and expectation. John tells us that they are stirred when Jesus says that he will draw all people to himself. This is an often-quoted passage, but note what it says in full: "And I, when I am lifted up from the earth, will draw all people to myself" (verse 32). John notes that Jesus said this to indicate his upcoming death. Jesus knew that the crowd would not follow him to the bitter end. In fact, he said that he will draw all people to himself—in future tense—only when he is lifted up from the earth. Only in Jesus' death and departure would people really be able to follow him. This is the paradox of following Jesus at a distance. It is only through his distance, his absence, when he is lifted up from the earth, that we are able to find his presence.

Jesus is always elusive. We can never be sure that we have properly followed him. Just when we get really close we find ourselves going the other way. Jesus did not come to bridge the gap between God and us, but to make the path through that gap clear. We follow Jesus because we know the distance is so great, because in Jesus we see not the glory but the suffering of God, a distance that beckons and demands but also warns us to count the cost of following. We do not follow at a distance, but rather we follow this distance, the mystery of the suffering God, who promises that our suffering, too, will one day be redeemed.

Prayer:

Lord God, teach us how best to follow you through the many detours of this life. We ask that you be patient when we stumble, and we ask for your understanding when we rush ahead, anxious and proud of how far we have come. Help us to follow you when we know not where we are going. Give us courage to continue our journey when we can see neither the beginning nor the end. Teach us to know when to wait and when to run. Give us the strength of weakness in order to partake of Jesus' suffering, even when we must do so at a distance.

Above all, remind us that we cannot make this journey alone. Let us pause to embrace those who cannot follow you, those without hope and those without help. And let us match our steps with those who suffer: people whose health, spiritual and physical, makes this journey especially difficult. Teach us that the way along this road is not a race or a contest but a daily lesson to practice a life of redemptive suffering. Let us embrace the very distance that Jesus traveled, even when we cannot follow him to the very end. Amen.

(SW)

15. Prayer
(Luke 15:11–32)

Our dear God, you are like a father to us yet we have sinned against you. We have taken our inheritance from you and have left your house and gone into a foreign land. We have squandered your gifts in our unwholesome desires for the things of this foreign world. And now we find ourselves impoverished and in the midst of famine. May we not be content to live in the squalor of this foreign world. May we now come to ourselves and remember that you are our home and that you still love us. Although we are like unworthy and prodigal sons, gather us back into your embrace. We repent and return to you still wearing our rags from a sinful world. O God, like a father, clothe us in a new robe that we may know your love for us. Give us shoes for our feet that we may know your constant care and concern for us. Put a ring on our hand that we may know your forgiveness. Dear God, we were dead. May we, in this bread and wine, know that you have made us alive again. We were lost. May we in this holy communion know that we have been found. Amen.

(KT)

16. Meditation and Litany

In Luke 22:14–20, Jesus shares bread and a cup with his disciples during the Passover meal and instructs them to "do this in remembrance of me." Although our intentions may be good, there are times when we fail to appreciate and understand the full impact of these six words.

To remember means, in part, to bring together pieces of a scattered or fragmented whole. The missing pieces of the puzzle are restored to their places. The blank spaces confronting us with the fact of incompletion are filled in. At the communion table, we cannot remember or be reminded in this deep sense until we speak and hear and feel the circumstances and details in the lives of Jesus and his disciples at that first communion meal.

Though it is painful and difficult, we must remember:
—the betrayal of trust and expectation;
—the pain of a broken body tortured to the point of death;
—the suffering of both the individual and the larger community when even one person's blood is shed;
—the anger and confusion and hatred of those who witnessed the betrayal and crucifixion of Jesus, whether a disciple or family member or a part of the religious or civil authorities.

Only when we remember those details and take them personally can we go beyond the suffering to claim the promises and victory that are ours, through Jesus:
—forgiveness of our sins;
—assurance of God's abiding love and compassion;
—participation in a community of faith and spirit that even death cannot destroy.

Prayer

As children of God and followers of Jesus, may we be more fully aware in these moments who it is and what it is we are preparing to remember. Then, may what we do and share be truly done "in remembrance."

Communion Litany:

Pastor: Hear these words from the prophet Isaiah: "Ho, everyone who thirsts, come to the waters; and you that have no money, come, buy and eat!" (Isaiah 55:1).

Elder: Likewise, we are invited to come eat and drink. We are invited to share in this feast of love and sacrifice.

Pastor: Jesus invites us to this table and welcomes us all, no matter who we are or where we've been.

Elder: Participation does not require an R.S.V.P. or fancy dress. There is a place at this table prepared for each of us, and all is in readiness.

Pastor: Jesus guarantees that any and all who hunger and thirst for spiritual nourishment may receive this bread of life broken for all and this cup of life poured out for all.

Elder: So come now, all you who hunger and thirst. Be welcome here as sisters and brothers of Jesus, the Christ, who gives us these gifts of love and promise and bids us receive them.

(AP)

17. Prayer Toward the End of Lent

Our dear God, we remember. We remember that the people of Israel wandered in the wilderness for forty years, but you gave them manna for bread. And we remember Noah. We remember that the terror of the storm raged about Noah for forty days and forty nights as he wandered in his watery wilderness. But you sustained Noah and upheld him on the face of the deep. We remember that Elijah wandered in the wilderness forty days, but you sustained him with the silent sound of your still, small voice. We remember that Jesus fasted in the wilderness for forty days, but was comforted by your angels.

Dear God, we now come near the end of these forty days of Lent. Many of us have wandered in our own personal wildernesses. Like Noah, keep us safe from the terror of our storms. Like Jesus, minister to us through your angel messengers. Like Elijah, sustain us in the silence of your presence, that in this wandering we may find rest. Like Israel, give us your bread, that in this wilderness we may find life. Amen.

(KT)

18. For Palm Sunday
(John 12:12–19)

For this Palm Sunday it seems right to look at Jesus as he himself is looking, at a distance. Jesus sees Jerusalem in the distance, and with Jerusalem he sees his own destiny. On his trip to Jerusalem Jesus closes the gap between his teaching ministry and its climactic resolution. The Gospels see this distance closed by means of the lowly donkey, and the closer Jesus gets to Jerusalem the more excited and anxious the people get about the hope that he is the king, the expected one, the Messiah.

It is difficult to put these events in the proper perspective. John, for example, says all of this in retrospect, with the advantage of hindsight. It is clear from the text that Jesus' contemporaries did not understand the distance that Jesus was to travel. Many greeted him with palm branches, honoring him as an earthly ruler, not understanding that he was journeying to meet his death and not glory. Even his very own disciples needed some distance from Jesus before they could properly focus their understanding of him. Only in their memories did this journey make sense. And yet many did try to follow him at this crucial stage in his journey. In fact, the Pharisees, in a bit of exaggeration, were worried that the whole world had gone after Jesus (verse 19). The crowds followed, but they were following so closely they could not see where they were going. The distance Jesus was covering would lead him to a lonely death, not a massive victory.

This pack of traffic heading for Jerusalem was bound to cause an accident. When the crucifixion put the brakes on Jesus' mission, those traveling close behind him would not have time to react. They would panic and crash and be dispersed in the disaster of the death of God.

Prayer:
Lord, help us in our need to have a God who does not die, a God who does not suffer, a life without pain or lack or want. We sometimes try to follow you so closely, thinking that in your company we can be safe from every harm. We are eager to forget that what you offer us is not easy consolation but the

blood and the body of a broken person, who has embraced our suffering at the ultimate cost. Forgive us for wanting to follow you only where we ourselves want you to go. Help us to read the signs that will point us along the proper way, the way in which you have found peace through struggling, love through pain, and life through death. Amen.

(SW)

19. For Palm Sunday

"But he was wounded for our transgressions, crushed for our iniquities; upon him was the punishment that made us whole, and by his bruises we are healed" (Isaiah 53:5).

Come to the table and remember the sacrifice.

Come to the table and remember the broken body and the shed blood.

Come to the table and be healed.

Prayer for the Bread:

O mighty God, in this bread we see the brokenness of your Son upon a cross. We remember the willingness with which he entered Jerusalem though to do so meant certain death. We call to mind the grace by which he offered forgiveness to his executioners, and pardon to the repentant thief beside him. Pour out your Spirit upon this bread that it might symbolize for us that broken body. Consecrate it with your blessing that as we eat, we might share in his suffering, and be united by his sacrifice. Grant that in the eating we might be strengthened to follow in his footsteps, even unto death. We pray this in Jesus' name. Amen.

Prayer for the Cup:

O loving God, in this cup we see the blood of Jesus Christ poured out for us. We call to mind his blood that was shed by the sting of a whip, the crown of thorns, a sword in his side. We remember the blood that poured from his brow as he agonized in that garden, and we remember his prayer, "Not my will but yours be done" (Luke 22:42). Pour out your Spirit upon this cup that it might be for us the blood of Christ shed for us. Grant that your Spirit may enter into us, that as we partake we might be given the mind of Christ to pray with him, not our own will but yours be done. In Jesus' name we pray. Amen.

(SM)

20. For Maundy Thursday

What a lonely night it was! Jesus was all alone—to face his decision—to face his accusers—to face his persecution—to face his death. Alone.

Oh, yes, he was surrounded by his disciples. They were there gathered around him in the upper room. They were there when he told of his betrayal by one of them. They were there as he prayed in the garden. They were there when he was arrested. But still he was all alone, for they did not see, they did not hear, they did not understand.

One would betray him. One would deny him. All would run away and hide. And he would be all alone—all alone to face his trial, his persecution, his crucifixion, his death.

What a lonely night it was. On the cross, he even felt abandoned by God: "My God, my God, why have you forsaken me?" (Matthew 27:46).

But it was not the end. His trial, his crucifixion, his death were not the end. We remember the sacrifice he made. We remember his lonely vigil, his fruitless efforts to reach the people, to reach his disciples. We remember, and we know it was not the end. For the end was life.

The end is a living presence to those who see and hear and understand. Jesus endured that lonely time that we might never have to be alone as he was.

When we face trials and temptations, we are not alone. When we face persecution, ridicule, even death, we are not alone. We come to the table, and we are not alone. For Christ is with us at this table and everywhere.

We do not have to be alone, for he walked through that lonesome valley of death—that we might never have to be alone. He endured that lonely sacrifice that we might know his presence, his strength, his courage.

Come, and remember. Come, and enjoy his presence. Come, and let Christ be with you. For he said, "Remember, I am with you always" (Matthew 28:20).

Prayer:

O God, giver of life and love, we wonder how we can ever thank you for the gift of a Savior. We wonder how we can ever measure up. For so often we give up. So often we say, "I can't."

We forget the lonely trial of Jesus and his lonely dying on the cross. We forget his promise to be with us. And so often we feel so alone.

Come, Holy Spirit, and be with us. Be with us as we take this bread. Be with us as we drink of this cup. Be with us as we remember the sacrifice of Jesus. Touch us with your love and forgiveness. Fill us with your courage and strength, that we might go from here fortified for service, strengthened by your presence.

Feed us at this table with power, with purpose, with presence, that we might not forget: we are never alone. Amen.

(DC)

21. Maundy Thursday Meditation

He gathered around the table for a festive meal with his friends. Suddenly, without warning, he got up from the table, wrapped a towel around his waist, took a basin of water and assumed the role of a servant washing the guests' dusty feet. His friends could barely stand it and protested loudly. Could it be that the man with wet hands and a damp towel did not understand the meaning of the Passover meal? Or could it be that he understood better than anyone else? Could it have been that he was telling them he would empty himself and take on the role of a servant even unto death for them, for us? Could it be that he was announcing that this meal, the water and the wine, would all too soon become a symbol of salvation, celebration, and call to servant ministry in his name?

(CDN)

Easter

Celebrating the Power
of Presence

E aster meant lambing season on my grandparents' farm. I
   would jump out of bed early in the morning, knowing that
Grandpa would let us kids accompany him to the sheep barn
where we would count the number of lambs born that day. As
a city kid, this miracle of life seemed magical and mysterious
to me, in part because I never actually saw a lamb being born.
Only once do I remember seeing the aftermath of a lamb's
birth. When I asked my grandfather where the blood came
from, he refused to answer. His uncharacteristic silence left
me wondering about the mystery of life.

I still wonder. My grandparents sold the farm and a few
years later my grandfather died. My grandmother, now ninety-
two, is full of life. I am no longer an innocent child, but I
marvel at the power of life, the miracle of new life, the renewal
of life through remembrance and the resurrection hope of
endless life.

Easter is a season of thanksgiving for the transforming
power of God in Christ who is ever-present throughout history, throughout Jesus' life, throughout our lives. It is not a
time to be silent about the mystery of life, but to celebrate it in

all its innocence and blood-stained birth. Communion during Easter remembers the women who jumped out of Jesus' tomb testifying to his new life. It is a time for us to celebrate the victory of the Lamb of God. It is lambing season.

1. For Easter Sunday

Once a pastor had the dilemma of convincing a parishioner that he could participate in communion. It seems the parishioner never felt he was worthy to partake in the loaf and the cup because of his sinful state. Before the Easter worship service, the pastor saw her friend in the narthex and inquired, "Will you take communion with us today?" The man shrugged his shoulders. The pastor responded, "It's Easter Sunday! Jesus died for your sins and is resurrected today so that you are made worthy of God. Your sins are forgiven! Isn't that worth having communion today?!"

Her friend made a decision on that particular Easter Sunday and at every worship service that followed. He finally recognized his worth in God's eyes during communion time. Do you?

(LRL)

Prayer:

O gentle Savior, risen Christ, teach us to listen for the speaking of our names. As Mary stood near the tomb expecting only the gardener, so we stand near the places of death unaware of your presence in our midst. Call our name, O Christ, that we may recognize the familiar love and assurance that brings new promise.

O living Christ, promised Savior, awaken our senses; stir us from the numbness that blurs our vision. As the disciples walked their grief-stricken road seeing only the stranger, so we journey in your presence unaware of the power in our midst. Be known to us, O Christ, in the breaking of the bread. Gather us in the power of your presence as we share the ordinary, only to be transformed by the holy. In the presence of the risen Christ we pray. Amen.

(JF)

2. Communion of the Newly Baptized

(When the service of the Lord's Supper is to follow baptism, as it often does during Eastertide, this liturgy may be used by the congregation and newly baptized sisters and brothers.)

Elder: Blessed One, you call us forth by name.
We come to you, your creatures,
returning to you as to streams of living water.
As Spirit, you hover over us as you moved
over the waters of creation.
As Creator, you call us into being in your image;
As Redeemer, you bring us, again and again, into
renewal and life.

Still wet with the waters of baptism, we come re-membering how you have always made safe passage for us, your people, through the waters of this world: how you sealed the family of Noah safely in the ark and signed your covenant of peace with them in rainbow mists;

how you brought the kinfolk of Miriam and Moses out of Egypt and made a way for them through the Reed Sea;
how you led the children of Israel across the Jordan into the promised land of milk and honey;

how you have established your dwelling with us, sheltering us in your tents and leading us beside still waters.

And so, with the community of drifters who have been found, led, and steadied by your hand, we join in thankful praise saying:

People: HOLY, HOLY, HOLY LORD, GOD OF POWER AND MIGHT.
HEAVEN AND EARTH FILL TO OVERFLOWING WITH
YOUR PRESENCE.
COME SAVE US BY YOUR HAND.
COME FEED US AT YOUR TABLE.
COME LEAD US TO YOUR PEACE.

(LPR)

3. Meditation and Prayers for Bread and Cup

Water flowing over parched ground brings forth life where all was dormant.
Leaven added to the dough causes bread to rise.
Wind in the sails propels a boat to its destination.
We know something's power by the change it causes.

In the resurrection of Jesus Christ, the power of God's presence changed things:
—like water on parched ground, it gives us new life;
—like leaven in the loaf, it fills us with quiet power to change the world;
—like wind, God's Spirit moves us toward our destiny.

Around the table to which Jesus invites all disciples,
we gather to celebrate the power of the risen Christ to change us.

Prayer for the Bread:
God, our provider,
    like a mother who prepares bread for her family,
    you have prepared this table for us.
In the gift of Jesus Christ,
    you turned starvation into salvation.
We are here because we choose life
    and give thanks for the abundance of your loving care.
We come humbly to the table,
    recognizing that in our sin we reject life.
So we come to partake of this loaf with petitions
    for forgiveness and renewing change.
Reform our intention and courage to do Christ's will.
In the name of him whose body was broken as the bread, Amen.

Prayer for the Cup:
God, our guide,
    like a wise father who knows how to prepare his family for a journey,
    you have prepared this cup.
In the desert of our lives,
    our thirst for righteousness is never-ending.
In the oasis of your love,
    we have no cause to fear.

We come to your table once again to partake of this cup of blessing.
We come in remembrance of Jesus
    and in faithful celebration of his sacrifice and victory.
With this cup, O God, fill us with the power of your presence
    until our lives overflow with joyful proclamation of the good news.
Hallelujah! Amen.

(MAP)

4. Communion Prayers

Prayer Before Communion:
    Holy God, in this celebration of new life, we give you thanks for your resurrection power. When your people were locked in the death of slavery, you offered them new life in a new land. When your people were forced away from their homes and into exile, you offered them new hope and vision through the words of your prophets. When we were condemned to death through the power of sin, you offered us new life through the death and resurrection of our Lord Jesus Christ. Yet today, when evil, apathy, and ignorance seem the order of the day, your Spirit breaks through as often as the lonely are comforted or the hungry fed.
    In these elements of bread and wine, offer to us your life-giving presence through the power of the Holy Spirit. Touch and bless these ordinary gifts that they may become for us the body and blood of Christ. Touch and bless us through these gifts that we may become for the world the body of Christ; witnesses to the resurrection.
    Strengthen us as we receive these gifts that in them we may find new life, new hope, and the power of the Easter story. We pray in the name of our resurrected Lord. Amen.

Prayer After Communion:
    We give you thanks, O loving God, for these undeserved gifts. For the bread and the cup that unite us with you and your Son through the power of the Holy Spirit, we offer our glad and grateful hearts. As we rise from this table, may you send us forth with a renewed spirit, strengthened and refreshed to bear witness to you. In Jesus' name we pray. Amen.

(SM)

5. Meditation

Took, blessed, broke, gave.

Those are very important words for us at the communion table. We remember those words Christ spoke when he shared his table of love with us. But this is not the only place we find these wonderful words.

Remember at the feeding of the multitude with the loaves and fishes? He took, he blessed, he broke, he gave. The disciples began to recognize Jesus as Lord.

Remember on the road to Emmaus, when he sat in the evening by the fire, to eat bread with the two disciples? He took, he blessed, he broke, he gave. They instantly recognized Jesus as the Christ.

When we gather around the table and hear the words: "He took, he blessed, he broke, he gave." How do we recognize Jesus?

(LRL)

6. Prayer

Gracious God, as we have journeyed through Lent, we have come to understand more fully what it means to say that this bread represents the body of the Christ, which was broken for us.

We are in awe as we consider the range of feeling we have seen in the last week:

—from the high of being treated like a king on Palm Sunday, to the low of being executed among thieves on Friday.

—from the fellowship of supper with friends, to the misunderstanding, desertion, betrayal, and denial by even the closest of friends.

We remember the false accusations, the mockery, the torture, the agony of a slow and painful death.

And for all of this, we give thanks because now we know that nothing we go through, not even broken relationships or death, is beyond your experience and understanding.

And then comes Easter morning, and we have learned that none of these things are beyond your reach—that nothing, not even death, can separate us from the love of Jesus Christ. And we want to say, "Hallelujah! Praise God!"

But God, in our joy, let us not forget that the cross is not only a symbol of redemption but also a symbol of sacrificial service—that we too are called to serve.

And now we can say: Amen.

(CE)

7. Meditation and Prayers for Bread and Cup

I am amazed that the tulips are blooming in my yard again. Amazed that they have survived the winter. Amazed that they thrive despite my care. I say despite because I'm really not much of a gardener. Yet somehow my well-intentioned efforts are enough for tulips to grow.

We read in Acts that "awe came upon everyone, because many wonders and signs were being done by the apostles" (Acts 2:43). The church was beginning to grow and generosity poured forth from the communion table. All was held in common, everyone ate with glad and generous hearts. They really had no idea what they were doing, but somehow their well-intentioned efforts were just enough for the church to grow.

This is the promise that draws us together around this table. Gathered together by this bread and this cup, our efforts to build community in the world will be enough. For the same power that shines upon the tulips at spring and blew into the generous hearts of those gathered around the table long ago is here in our midst. Isn't it amazing?

Prayer for the Bread:
Good Shepherd, we gather around this table to break bread together. In this moment of communion gather us together into one flock united in purpose to care for the world as you have cared for us. With grateful hearts we pray. Amen.

Prayer for the Cup:
Lamb of God, in this cup we see the strength of your righteousness poured out upon the world. We stand in awe of the one who suffered, but did not threaten; who was abused, but did not return abuse. Pour upon us the power to meet evil with justice, so that we might live for righteousness. In the name of the one who is guardian of our souls, we pray. Amen.

(JM)

8. Prayer

We come to your table with joy, O God, a joy and expectation like that with which we welcome the coming of spring when the warm sun and the cleansing rain dispel all traces of ugliness and make way for the burst of new life.

In the light of your presence, we are able to see and understand the ugliness of our lives—the broken relationships, the conflicting priorities, the faithless loyalty, the unproductive obligation, the self-centeredness—and we are able to envision lives motivated by singleness of purpose and purity of heart.

In the power of your presence, we are able to act, to become new beings, to risk, to give of ourselves for others. As we partake of this bread and cup, we pray for forgiveness for what we have been and now leave behind, and the power to know and to do your will. We pray in the name of Jesus, in whose name we celebrate this communion. Amen.

(VL, from *The Gifts We Bring,* Vol. 2)

9. Communion Prayers

Prayer Before Communion:

O Holy One, we come humbly to the table of sacrifice... broken, confused, and afraid. In need of your blessing we stand, always aware of your promise to receive us into fellowship in spite of our restlessness and rebellion. Listen now to the confessions of our hearts. Be keenly aware of the inner longings of our spirits that only you can fulfill. Heal our brokenness by the memory of your own pain suffered on our behalf. Break the bonds of fear and confusion that often haunt us by the presence of your power in the meal set before us. Now, O Christ, take our weary spirits and breathe new life into them as we remember with gratitude all you have done for us. Amen.

Prayer After Communion:

Refreshed and renewed, O Christ, we emerge from communion with you, no longer broken by our confusion and fear. We are now living loaves reshaped by your grace and forgiveness. We are now fresh-flowing wine, ready to be poured out in celebration of your life-giving Spirit. We are whole once again and we praise you for the transformation. Through Jesus our Lord, we pray. Amen.   (KEW)

10. Prayer and Response

Elder: Blessed One, who names us and steadies us, we have heard
how you joined us in the waters of Mary's womb;
how you grew and traveled here among us;
how you were baptized by your servant John.
We rejoice that you joined the wedding feast at Cana, turning water into wine.
We grieve that you faced death on Calvary.
We would join the woman who washed your feet with her tears.

By your death and resurrection, you have brought us safe through the waters once more, and so we join all who have been given safe passage into life, proclaiming the mystery of the faith:

People: CHRIST HAS DIED;
CHRIST IS RISEN;
CHRIST WILL COME AGAIN!

(LPR)

11. Litany and Prayer
(1 Peter 2:1–10)

One: "I am laying in Zion a stone, a cornerstone chosen and precious."

Many: WE COME TO YOU, O BREAD OF LIFE.
MAKE US LIVING STONES.

One: "Whoever believes in him will not be put to shame."

Many: WE COME TO YOU, O LIVING VINE.
MAKE US LIVING STONES.

Elder: O God, our rock and our salvation, we come before you gathered around this banquet table, hungry for your mercy, which is the cornerstone of our lives. May this bread be for us the bread of life. May we be the living stones of your spiritual house. May this cup be for us a living vine. May we be a holy priesthood, your own people. Indeed, you have called us out of darkness and into light. May we grow in the light of your salvation. Amen.

(JM)

12. Meditation and Prayer

"And the angel said to me, 'Write this: Blessed are those who are invited to the marriage supper of the Lamb'" (Revelation 19:9).

John the Divine, the one who communicated his magnificent vision of the close of this age and the opening of God's new age to seven churches in Asia Minor, reports only his beatitude upon those invited to the marriage feast. His vision does not include a glimpse of the feast itself. Heavenly choirs sing of the preparation of the bride, the community that has been faithful to the Lamb, and the worthiness of the bridegroom. But never are we allowed to see the table spread with an abundance of every kind of delicious food and drink. Nor do we smell their aroma, nor taste the sweet and sour, the salt and bland of each dish prepared for the banquet. And we do not hear the clatter of dishes and the ring of silverware, chattering voices and congratulatory toasts sung out in praise of the host. The warmth of the room does not caress our skin; the affectionate embraces of the guests and their host are never felt.

Of course, the fact that the banquet is not depicted is not due to any lack of John's descriptive powers. With rich and varied imagery, John is able to draw us into other parts of his grand vision. We can nearly see, smell, taste, hear, and feel the doom of the four approaching horsemen as the first seals are broken, the terrors of the destruction of the cosmos in the blasts of trumpets and the upturning of bowls, the grief over a lost civilization that had finally curled inward upon itself. Through a catena of lovely images at the end, John is even able to offer a glimpse of the final union between God and God's beloved creation, when wounds are healed by the leaves of the tree of life, hunger assuaged by its fruits, and tears dried by God, God's self. But not a word is uttered beyond the beatitude: "Blessed are those who are invited to the marriage feast of the Lamb."

Maybe, just maybe, John knew what we also know, that the closest thing we have to that marriage feast of our future is the common table spread before us now. Mere words cannot express what this cup and this loaf signify: the foretaste of the messianic banquet when all who say that Jesus is Lord will be ushered into the best seats in the house. In our gathering around this table, may we also bless our world with an invitation to participate in the feast, both this one and the one that is to come.

(NCP)

Prayer:

O God, that was and is and is to come, we gather around this banquet table, a foretaste of your glory divine. With those of old we are strengthened by this table of righteousness where all are honored, all are fed. With those present throughout the world today we are encouraged by this table of fellowship that binds us together in life-shaping ministry. With those to come we are challenged by this table of celebration whose ultimate victory we are promised to share. We gather around this banquet table, a foretaste of your glory divine. Come, Lord Jesus, come. Amen.

(JM)

13. Litany and Unison Prayer

Elder: Come now, Spirit and creating God:
Knead this bread into the body of Christ among us.

People: FEED US FOR OUR JOURNEY.

Elder: Come now, Spirit and redeeming Lord:
Pour into this cup Christ's generous love.

People: SLAKE OUR THIRSTING SOULS.

Elder: Come now, Spirit and safe-keeping Friend:
Flood our hearts with peace.

People: FILL OUR LIVES WITH STRENGTH AS WE PARTAKE OF THIS FEAST IN JESUS' NAME, REMEMBERING HIS SUPPER WITH THOSE WHO TRAVELED WITH HIM.

Unison: BLESSED ONE, WHO NAMES US AND STEADIES US
AND NOURISHES US,
WE CELEBRATE YOUR PRESENCE WITH US
THROUGH THE WATER AND THE WORD.
BY YOUR REDEEMING LOVE, YOU HAVE WASHED US.
BY YOUR CREATING POWER, YOU HAVE REFRESHED US.
BY YOUR SUSTAINING SPIRIT,

YOU HAVE QUENCHED OUR THIRST.
SWELL OUR HEARTS WITH FAITH AND LOVE,
AND SEND US NOW INTO THE WORLD. AMEN.

(LPR)

14. Meditation

Once there was a man who was so authoritative in his words and authentic with his life that he himself seemed to be God. God was in his words. He was often heard to say, "You have heard it said...but I say to you." He told stories and they were words of the Kingdom.

God was in his life; he lived his brief days with the highest moral integrity and the deepest spirituality. There was healing in his touch, compassion in his eyes, love in his heart.

God was in his death, when all he had to give in life was still not enough. We gather at this table to be challenged by the example of his authentic life and to seek to live by that example and, when that is not enough, to give thanks that by his death and resurrection we are given a chance to begin anew.

(CDN)

15. Prayers for Bread and Cup
(John 17:20–26)

Prayer for the Bread:

Holy One, we come to this table longing for the taste of your wholeness in the broken morsels of our lives. In the midst of family arguments and workplace tensions we long for your healing presence. Despite the discord of our society and the fraction of your church we cling to your vision that we may be one even as you are one. As we partake of this bread, symbol of unity, may we be strengthened in communion with you and with one another. Amen.

Prayer for the Cup:

Loving One, we raise this cup to lips parched by the lonely deserts of our lives. As we drink of your vision of community an oasis of possibility stands before our eyes. We see hope flow into our families, our church, our daily lives. We envision waters of love filling the chasms that separate us from one another. We experience the ever-flowing-streams of your grace, which unite us in the fountain of salvation. As we partake of this cup we join in your prayer that "we may become completely one." Amen.

(JM)

16. Meditation and Prayer

(John 15:12–17)

We often come around this table heavy with the burden of sacrifice endured for our sake, weary of the responsibility of servanthood. The debt that we cannot repay bears down upon our lives. Could we lay down our lives, love as we have been loved? Impossible.

And yet Jesus proclaims that in God's eyes we are not servants, but friends. We are not called to a life of blind obedience, but of knowledgeable collaboration. Freed from the burden of earning divine love, we can be appointed to bear fruitful witness to God's love in the world. We are here to participate in a love freely given, freely shared. Let us cast aside our guilt, our sense of obligation. Let us feast together, joined by our Host and our Friend.

Prayer:

Our heavenly Friend, with glad rejoicing we come to this communion table. Bread of love is freely broken in your presence. Outpouring love flows in this wine. As we receive this communion, words cannot express the depth of love that swells in our hearts. We are honored by your presence. We are humbled by your friendship. We are challenged by your witness. May we be empowered to follow your example. May we love one another as friends. Amen.

(JM)

Pentecost

Sharing in the
Presence of Power

While I have been working on this collection I have also been involved in renovating the church parsonage where I live. The parsonage is a grand house, built in the 1920s, but it had lost a considerable amount of its grandeur in recent years. There was a lot of talk about selling the place. After all, the location wasn't the best, and the amount of work needed to fix it up was almost more than the church trustees could contemplate.

But before the house could be sold, it had to be repainted. In a moment of madness one trustee suggested, "Let's paint it ourselves." The following Saturday forty people showed up to paint. The event transformed the congregation. People were amazed at what they had accomplished together. There was no more discussion of selling the house. Instead people turned their attention to the next project, reglazing the windows.

For a few months the house stood vacant while a small group worked quietly behind the scenes. Then a burst of energy swept over the congregation and in the course of six weeks the redecorating was completed. Each day I would delight in going to the parsonage, partly out of curiosity to see what had been done. But mostly I just wanted to be there and be a part of this transformative spirit.

Finally, my family moved in. We had an open house and the congregation took pride in a job well done. The church members, however, were not done. They had caught a glimpse of the power of their collective spirit. Now they are looking beyond themselves with new visions of mission to the community.

They have caught that Pentecost spirit, that active involvement in the ongoing presence of God's power in the church and throughout the world. During communion we need to lift up the ordinary efforts of our community to deal with the ordinary problems of life and celebrate the extraordinary way our efforts are transformed in God's service.

1. For Pentecost Sunday

(Written for the Kentuckiana Disciples Area Pentecost Service, Louisville, Kentucky, June 7, 1992.)

Invitation to Communion:

In the International Headquarters of the Christian Church (Disciples of Christ) in Indianapolis, there is a chapel open to all employees and visitors. The pulpit, lectern, and communion table in this chapel were made of over two thousand five hundred pieces of wood. The wood came from all over the world—from mission stations, local churches, colleges and seminaries, even the Cane Ridge Meeting House. Fashioned together by a master craftsman, the individual pieces were formed into beautiful furniture used to worship and praise God.

Like those pieces of wood, we too come to the table as individuals, each with our own story to tell. We come from different lifestyles, different communities, different histories. But when we come to this table, we are joined together by the loving hands of our Master Crafter; we are formed into one community, united by the blood and body of our Lord Jesus.

As we partake of the bread and cup this day, may we allow God to form us into one body, joined by one Spirit, and united in service to the one Lord. And in that unity, may we be used in worship and in praise.

Prayer for the Bread and Cup:

Pastor: The Lord be with you.

People: AND ALSO WITH YOU.

Pastor: Lift up your hearts.

People: WE LIFT THEM TO THE LORD.

Pastor: Let us give thanks to the Lord our God,

People: IT IS RIGHT TO GIVE THANKS AND PRAISE.

Pastor: It is right, and a good and joyful thing, always and everywhere to give thanks to you, Lord God Almighty, Creator of heaven and earth.

Elder 1: In the beginning your Spirit moved across the waters and called forth life from death and order from chaos. When your people Israel were enslaved, your Spirit led them forth to freedom and into a new land. At the baptism of our Lord, your Spirit descended like a dove, blessing and consecrating him and guiding him throughout his ministry. In the dark hours before his crucifixion, Jesus promised the gift of the Comforter, the Holy Spirit, to lead and guide for the ages to come. After the resurrection, Jesus was made known to his friends in the breaking of the bread, and in that bread and cup your Spirit continues to move.

Elder 2: On the day of Pentecost your Spirit came with the sound of a mighty wind and the appearance of tongues of fire to fill the apostles with grace and power, sending them out to preach the good news of your gracious love in Christ Jesus. Throughout the ages, your Spirit has moved to touch the lives of your children and to anoint them for witness and service. So in this communion service today, may your Spirit again move and bless these elements, the bread and the cup. May these simple, ordinary gifts become for us the body and blood of Christ, that as we go forth into the world, we may be the body of Christ united by his blood.

Pastor: It is with glad and joyful hearts that we receive these gifts, remembering how on the night that Jesus was betrayed, he took bread...*(Insert words of institution from one of the Gospels or 1 Corinthians.)*

As we partake of this bread and drink of this cup, may we remember the sacrifice of our Lord, and the salvation he offered. May we be filled with a fresh anointing of the Holy Spirit to go forth praising God. May we be revived and refreshed, recommitted to witnessing to God's gracious love in both word and deed. It is in Jesus' name that we pray. Amen.

Prayer of Thanksgiving, After Communion:

Unison: WE GIVE YOU THANKS, MOST GRACIOUS GOD,
FOR THE GIFTS WE HAVE RECEIVED:
—FOR THE GIFT OF THE HOLY SPIRIT THAT CONTINUES TO BLOW THROUGH OUR WORLD;
—FOR THE WITNESS OF CHRISTIANS EVERYWHERE WHO ARE TOUCHED BY YOUR SPIRIT;
—FOR THE GIFTS OF BREAD AND CUP, WHICH ARE LIVING SYMBOLS OF YOUR GRACIOUS LOVE FOR US.
OPEN OUR EYES THAT WE MAY SEE,
OUR EARS THAT WE MAY HEAR,
OUR HEARTS THAT WE MAY RECEIVE,
SO THAT OUR LIVES MAY BEAR WITNESS TO YOU.
IN THE NAME OF THE RISEN LORD, OUR SAVIOR, WE PRAY.
AMEN.

(SM)

2. Meditation for Pentecost Sunday

Many of us have grown up with a strange sense that holy communion is a private matter—something between me and God—and not to be interrupted by the sound and movement of others. Even our decision making in the church about our communion procedures has often centered on what *I* want. Majority votes have carried the day, with little concern for the spiritual nourishment of the whole congregation.

The truth is that the act of holy communion is an act of relationship—the relationship between God, ourselves, and those with whom we gather around the table. It is an act that binds us to those in other places and times who will break this bread and drink from this cup. Bread blessed, broken, and given. Wine poured and shared with others. When we take a place at this table, it is an act of covenant love.

On the day of Pentecost, all who gathered were filled with the Holy Spirit and the divisions of Babel were set aside. Languages were spoken so that each could hear and understand the other. The church was gathered into being. If the breaking of this bread and the sharing of this cup are to be holy communion in Christ, then the barriers that have been used to divide the church must be broken down and cast aside. The fears that have bound our hearts will no longer be given power over our lives. Language that alienates will be exchanged for the Word that makes us one. A solitary act of eating and drinking will be transformed into communion in the body of Christ. Come to the table!

(JF)

3. Prayer for the Cup

O Spirit,
who bursts forth in our lives,
filling us as this cup is filled,
with the sweetness
of perfectly ripened fruit,
We thank you for this sign:
the container filled and emptied
and refilled.

You enter us and fill us,
and we enter again
the womb of life.

You empty yourself
in our new birth
and we empty ourselves
in service.

We drink with a thirst for water
and more than water:
We require a spirit
that can fill the world.
And we are filled.

(CC)

4. Meditation and Prayers for Bread and Cup

One of the things that is so reassuring about our faith is its balance. We have just celebrated Pentecost and the gift of the Holy Spirit, symbolized by tongues of flame, rushes of wind, and speaking in foreign languages. But here we are, being brought back to the realities of physical life on our earth by the impending wheat harvest, by the long, sunny, summer days that bring a special brightness to our lives, by the sneezes of hay fever, and by the laughter of children and the corresponding giggles of the teachers as they prepare for vacation Bible school. And I lift my voice in thanksgiving that we are both physical and spiritual beings and that God said, "It is good."

Here at the communion table, as well, we celebrate the spiritual presence of the living Christ with good, solid, physical symbols like a loaf of bread and a cup filled with the juice of grapes. And as we remember and give thanks for the gift of new life and new covenant, we also go forth with a renewed awareness of God's creation, so that as we pass a field of grain or see a jar of grape juice in the supermarket or feel the warm sunshine on our shoulders, it reminds us of God's enduring love.

Tongues of flame were miraculous and wonderful, but I'm awfully glad Jesus chose bread and grape juice as the symbols through which we are reminded of his love and his presence with us.

Prayer for the Bread:
God of life and love, we give you thanks for this loaf, through which we remember Christ's gift to us—his very body—that we might know eternal life. And we remember also the sunlight and the grain that was gathered together to make the loaf. Gather us also from the fields of our scattered lives and knead us together until we, too, become one loaf, one community of faith, living in the sunlight of your love.

Prayer for the Cup:
We give thanks as well, O God, for this cup, which reminds us of the shed blood of our Savior, that our lives might be cleansed and renewed. Strengthen us, we pray, that we may ever be willing to honor the new covenant he made with us and to share our lives with others as he did with us. Amen.

(MB)

5. Prayer for the Cup
(Holy Wisdom)

We gather at a table
set by Holy Wisdom,
to drink a wine
poured by Wisdom's own hands.

We come as a people called:
some from life's broad place,
others from life's nooks and crannies,
all too aware
of the personal pain
and communal fractures
that make us less than whole.

And yet we come giving thanks:
Thanks for the wisdom
of this dark liquid
that, dissolving fractures,
makes us whole;
Thanks for the wisdom
of this one cup
that, shared by us,
makes us one.

(CC)

6. Meditation

Look into this cup you hold. What do you see? A tiny pool
of dark liquid, still, cool to your touch through the cup walls.
Perhaps where you sit it reflects some light, from a window or
from a lamp overhead. Perhaps, if you turn your head just
right, you can see your own reflection in it, tiny as it is. In a
moment you will drink it, and it will become part of you, your
flesh and blood. For the moment, it is still apart from you. Is it
any different with Jesus? He is apart from us. It is difficult to
grasp him, and when we manage to do so, it always seems to
be in such small ways. Yet by this meal, as in so many other
ways, we take Christ into ourselves, and let him become part
of us. And, if we look closely enough, we just might see ourselves reflected in him. Come now, eat and drink, and let
Christ Jesus be one with you.

(DW)

7. Prayer for the Cup

Unbounded Spirit,
Teach us your ways!
The way of the cup,
containing what cannot be contained:
The firm exterior,
cradled in our hands as we drink,
like the earth on which we stand,
cradled in your arms.
The rounded interior,
source of life,
ever emptied
and ever refilled.
The mystery of its contents:
fruit of the earth,
life in our veins.

And you,
somehow present
not by magic,
nor yet merely as symbol:
Known by us deeply
in our partaking,
But known most powerfully
in our sharing!

Unbounded Spirit!
For this body
whose life you have become,
we give thanks.
We call forth your presence
in each passing of this cup,
And implore you:
Teach us your ways!

(CC)

8. Meditation and Prayer

Have you ever noticed how the communion symbols, bread
and wine, are made? For bread, you grow the wheat and
harvest it. Then you grind the grain until it is a fine flour. You

add your ingredients to the flour and start kneading it, pounding it and then gently letting it rise. Put it in the oven, and at a precise time it turns into a beautifully brown loaf of bread.

Vineyards take many years to grow correctly. Pruned at the right time, the vines can bring a bountiful harvest. When the grapes are ripe, they're picked. Then they are placed in a vat and broken and crushed until all the juice is taken from the fruit. Then, with special ingredients added, it is placed in a bottle for a time to ferment. The bottle of wine, when ready, has a flavor all its own.

Isn't it interesting that from crushed wheat and broken grapes, a whole loaf of bread and whole grape juice are made? How interesting it is that a broken people from a broken world can come to this table of Christ's love and be whole.

(LRL)

Prayer:

We thank you God for your continuing presence in our midst and especially as we gather at this table where you come to be present with us in a very special way. We come at your invitation and open ourselves to your welcome.

Here at this table, you offer us food—not to strengthen our bodies, but to nourish our spirits. Like a mother, you recognize our needs and understand our fears; you enthusiastically receive and forgive us as the father in the parable welcomed home a prodigal son. When we feel the love and fellowship of our closest friends, we recognize your love entering our lives through the gift of relationships.

As we prepare to receive this holy meal, we thank you for the many things you offer in the form of bread broken and a cup poured: love and courage to break down barriers of isolation; power to overcome our feelings of powerlessness; promises of new life in every new day; promises of strength for tired minds, bodies, and spirits; and your assurance of victory to all who trust and follow you.

As we share this meal together, empower us to embrace one another as members of your human family, that we may truly be a community of faith and instruments of peace and renewal in your world. Amen.

(AP)

9. Prayer for the Bread
(Jeremiah 17:7–11; Luke 6:17–26)

We would like to give thanks, O God,
for your promise to probe our hearts,
to know us as we know not ourselves.

We would like to give thanks
for your promise to bless the poor
and fill the hungry.
But we fear the light shed on our self-deceit,
and we know we are not poor.

We choke on our words of thanks for all we have
in the presence of the world's pain and need.

But for this broken loaf
we can indeed give thanks:
for this sign of the brokenness that mirrors our own,
as individuals and communities.

And we give thanks for the promise
that beyond brokenness
lie healing and transformation,
the possibility of coming before your presence
with thanksgiving,
in the kinship of all creation.

Let us taste your Spirit
in the broken loaf,
And with it the knowledge
that your body is made whole
in our bodies.
Plant us by your water this day!

(CC)

10. Prayer for the Cup
(Jeremiah 1:4–10)

Life-giver! Life-shaper!
We come this morning
with hearts full of thanks
for your creative work:

For the world
that you have brought to birth in wisdom;
For the church
that you have brought forth in justice;
For our very lives
touched by you already
as we were woven in the womb.

We come also aware
that our joy in the life you have given
Is often matched
by our resistance to your call.
Too often we pray
Jesus' *other* prayer:
"Let this cup pass from me."

But here indeed is the cup
you set before us:
the cross of love
in and for your world;
To seek our vocation
not just as individuals,
but as the people of God
in the world.

As we drink this cup,
pour forth your Spirit upon us,
And shape us as your church!
Give us vision and strength
that together
we may shape your world
in shalom.

(CC)

11. Litany for Communion

A Prayer Remembering the Work of God in Creation:

Elder: Holy, holy, holy Lord, above us and within,
you have fan-folded creation around us and
you open it out before us.
Throughout the reality of our unseen past and
in the possibilities we see ahead, you surround us.
In the history of Israel, we have seen your presence;
in the hope of the early Christian community,
we have heard your voice;
in the home of today's church,
we have been welcomed by your hospitality.
Holy, holy, holy Lord, above us and within;
around us and before us; behind us and ahead,
we join all your creatures always and everywhere,
saying:

People: HOLY, HOLY, HOLY LORD, GOD OF HOSTS.
HEAVEN AND EARTH ARE FULL OF YOUR GLORY.
HOSANNA IN THE HIGHEST!
BLESSED IS THE ONE WHO COMES IN THE NAME OF THE LORD.
HOSANNA IN THE HIGHEST!

A Prayer Remembering the Work of God in Christ:

Elder: Presently gathered here with your eternal family
at the table you prepare,
we remember today how you responded
to our hurt and hunger in Jesus Christ.
In your holiness, you are separate,
yet in Christ you are present among us.
In Christ's childlike playfulness,
our hearts are lightened;
by Christ's compassionate care-giving,
our wounds are healed;
through Christ's rebellious resistance to wrong,
we are challenged to oppose injustice;
and by Christ's steadfast compliance with ancient
wisdom,
we are called to faithful life and witness.
Joining all who have learned to tell the story of your

child, Jesus, who is our Christ,
we proclaim the mystery of the faith:

People: CHRIST HAS DIED;
CHRIST HAS RISEN;
CHRIST WILL COME AGAIN.

A Prayer Invoking the Holy Spirit:

Elder: Send now your Spirit on us and on these gifts of
bread and cup.
May they be for us the remembering of the Holy One
by whom our thirst is quenched and our hunger
satisfied.
Even as we tear the bread,
may it be textured with your love.
Even as we pour the wine [cup],
may it be the blood of new life,
pulsing among us and warming the world.

Words Of Institution

A Prayer Following the Supper:

Unison: HOLY, HOLY, HOLY LORD, ABOVE US AND WITHIN,
YOU HAVE GIVEN US A TASTE OF WHOLENESS;
YOU HAVE DRAWN US BY THE AROMA OF YOUR SPIRIT;
YOU HAVE NOURISHED AND RECREATED US.
SEND US NOW INTO THE WORLD TO EXTEND THE WELCOME
BY WHICH YOU WELCOMED US IN JESUS CHRIST,
THROUGH THE HOLY SPIRIT,
WITH YOU, ONE GOD, NOW AND FOREVER.
AMEN.

(LPR)

12. Meditation

(While holding up bread and considering it slowly and reverently:)
They say you are what you eat.

(CDN)

13. Meditation and Prayer

Early one morning, the young daughter of a good friend ran into the den, where he was reading the morning paper and announced that she wanted some cereal. It was quite a bit earlier than she was usually awake and he teasingly asked her, "Well, do you think your tummy is awake enough yet to eat?" She hesitated a minute and answered, "I don't know, Daddy, but my heart is hungry."

We all have hungry hearts—hearts that long for meaning, love, relationships, newness in life. A hungry heart, like a hungry stomach, signifies life and vitality. Here at the communion table we find sustenance for our hungry hearts, realizing that it is God who gives us the hunger, as well as the food to satisfy our hunger. Yet even as we celebrate eating of the bread of life and drinking the cup of the new covenant, we anticipate the rise of new hungers, and give thanks for them as well in the continuing spiritual journey of our hungry hearts. Jesus has prepared the table for us. All who believe in him are invited to his table.

(The story is from Dr. Mark Luera, minister of education at Midway Hills Christian Church, Dallas, Texas.)

Prayer:

We come to the table, O God, eager for the bread of life you offer, for our hearts are indeed hungry. We come in thanksgiving for the nourishment and renewed energy of spirit that has come to us through the very body of Christ Jesus. Help us, we pray, to remember that, as our own lives are filled with your grace, we are called to share the bread with our neighbors so that all who hunger and thirst for you may be filled.

As we share the cup of the new covenant, O God, we humbly open ourselves to the new life you prepare for us. Help us always to welcome the new hungers and thirsts you prepare for us, that we may not just remember the Christ who has come or celebrate the Christ who is with us now, but that we may also lean with faith into the future, anticipating the Christ who is yet to come and link our lives with his as together we journey in service and love. Amen.

(MB)

14. Meditation and Prayer

As chaplain of a women's maximum security prison, I am reminded of two words: imprisoned and free. My church consists of convicted women who are imprisoned. But the faithful Christians here will tell you they are more free since they found Jesus on the "inside" while living in prison on the "outside."

All of us have been in prison: the prison of sin, selfishness, and evil. The Lord's Table is the place where Jesus removes the shackles of sin and frees us to be reconciled with God. "Come to me, all you that are weary and are carrying heavy burdens, and I will give you rest" (Matthew 11:28). Come and eat this bread of life and drink this cup of salvation! Come and be free!

Prayer for the Bread:

Gracious God, help us to remember the power of your grace in this table of love. Remind us that it was the grace of your Son, Jesus Christ, to come into this world and take our sins upon himself. As we say grace over this loaf of bread, we remember the grace of each meal: a communion given from your heart and a sustenance of food to help us live your Word each day. As we partake of this spiritual sustenance, we thank you for your never-ending forgiveness, and as we live by your grace, let this bread symbolize the Christ that lives in us, so we may share his love with others. Amen.

Prayer for the Cup:

Creator God of all life, we thank you for this beautiful day as it resonates your presence in the breeze through the trees, the songs of nature, and in the night, the twinkling of the stars. As we come to this table, help us to remember the covenants you have made with your people for life, faith, and hope. In the drinking of this cup, we celebrate the new covenant from Jesus, a covenant of the forgiveness of our sins. As he has forgiven us, may we forgive others, with his compassion to help us build a new covenant of love. For it is in his name and in this community of love we celebrate communion this day. Amen.

(LRL)

15. Communion Meditation

There is an absurdity at this table.
In the midst of a world out to get him,
In the midst of criticism and accusations,
While people prepare his arrest and his trial,
Jesus gathers in a quiet upper room
For a quiet supper with his friends.
And there he reverently breaks bread
And blesses the cup and passes it around.
In that hour he blesses their lives,
While the hubbub, the hassle, the horror
Wait just beyond the door.

There is an absurdity at this table.
In the midst of personal crises and gloom,
In a world filled with disappointment and despair,
Where dreams may vanish into vapor,
And the world seems to crumble all around,
While hunger and heartache haunt the hopeless,
People gather at a quiet table in churches,
In storefronts, in crowded rooms, and in humble huts,
And there they break the bread and bless the cup
And remember the one who died for them.
And in this hour he blesses their lives.

There is an absurdity at this table.
While our minds race from crisis to crisis,
And we grapple with plans for getting ahead,
While we nurse our recent injuries,
And try to forget our worries and pressures,
We gather around a table almost bare and
In the midst of all life's hassles and horrors,
We break the bread and bless the cup.
Our lives are blessed; our minds are hushed;
In this hour he blesses our lives,
And somehow we see eternity.

                                                          (DC)

16. Meditation on the Table

There is a Disciples congregation in North Carolina that took great care in learning what the Lord's Supper meant to its people. They had finished building the sanctuary and were deciding what kind of church furniture to order. They looked in all the big-name church furniture catalogs. They looked at all the Lord's Tables: ones that had "Do this in remembrance of me" engraved in the front or had elaborate carvings of wheat tares and grapes or had different crosses, but not one of the tables suited anyone. Then something happened. They started talking among themselves about the meaning of communion. After all, isn't that the center of the Disciples worship? They talked of how the Lord's Supper was a family affair. Everyone had a place at this table of love. It seemed communion was the place where the whole church, in its greatest love, came together. Then they knew. They finally realized what they needed.

Do you know what they bought to symbolize the Lord's Table? Think about it. Where is the place the family comes together to eat a meal? The place where love is celebrated by a child who gently prays his or her first prayer, "God is great. God is good. Let us thank God for God's food. By God's hands we all are fed. Give us Lord our daily bread."

To this day a simple dining room table is the place where the bread of life and the cup of salvation are found in this church. Come. Come to Christ's dining room table of love.

(LRL)

17. Prayer
(1 Kings 17)

Dear God, we remember that you sent your prophet Elijah to a poor widow to be fed. We remember that although she herself was starving, in faith she shared all of her food with the prophet. Because of her faith her meager amount of meal was not used up and her small amount of oil did not fail. She and her household and the prophet ate of it for many days. As we gather around this table may we, like the widow, not be afraid to share all that we have—both physical and spiritual. May we have faith that, like the widow's meal, this bread that we break will never be used up and, like the widow's oil, this cup that we bless will never fail. Amen.

(KT)

18. Meditation on the Table

In drawing and drafting, your focal point is your reference for everything you do. Look around here: the focal point of this sanctuary is a table. All that we do here centers on and proceeds from this table and what takes place here. All the rest of the things that decorate our worship, such as crosses, musical instruments, windows, banners, even walls and ceiling, could be stripped away, and as long as this table remained, we would still have a focus for our worship. Indeed, even if the table itself were to vanish, leaving only the elements of bread and wine, we would still have our focus. That is how central, how vital, this sacrament is, this supper of the Lord. Let it draw the attention of your eyes, let it draw your heart. Together now, let us all come to Christ's Table, share his feast, and so join in full and true worship.

(DW)

19. Prayer

Creative God, source and sustainer of life,
we praise you for establishing earth and sky
as the means of companionship with you.
In sorrow we confess that because of our sin
the world is despoiled
and we no longer use it to enjoy life with you.
Merciful God, we give you thanks for Jesus Christ,
the one great sacrament of your love,
who forgives our sins, renews the earth,
and reestablishes relationships with you.

All of this we remember with thanksgiving
as we bring bread and wine
and other signs of our life to the communion table.
By your Word and Holy Spirit, bless us and these gifts
that Jesus' own words may be fulfilled:
    My body given for you.
    My blood of the covenant poured out for you.
Send us from this house of worship
ready to use the world once again as you intend,
as the means of joyful communion with you and one another.
Through Jesus Christ we pray. Amen.

(KW)

20. Meditation/Children's Sermon
(1 Corinthians 10:15)

"As the grain scattered across the fields has been gathered in this loaf, gather us as one in this broken bread." (From the *Didache*)

Materials Needed: One (or even two) bread machines, ingredients for bread. If a bread machine is not available, use a loaf of bread as fresh from the oven as possible, the hotter the better!

To Proceed: Gather the children around and ask them if they have ever seen a bread machine before. Show them all the ingredients and have the children mix them (or pass them around to examine if you are "just looking.") As the children handle each ingredient, talk about each one and what it does for the bread. What if we left out the yeast (or other leavening)? The loaf would be flat; yeast makes it fluff up. What about the water? The water makes it sticky so that when it bakes, the loaf won't crumble into little dry pieces. How about the salt? It makes it taste better. And so on. (If done with adults, the ingredients can be presented by a member who then describes what that ingredient does for the bread.)

After the ingredients are mixed, hold the bowl or give it to an adult who can finish the bread in the kitchen if that is your plan. Talk briefly about how all the "different stuff" goes into bread, but it comes out as one loaf. And if anything gets left out, the bread will not be as good. A long time ago a man named Paul told the church he worked with that being the people of the church was kind of like mixing a loaf of bread— lots of different things go in, but it all comes out as one bread. It takes all kinds of different people to make a church, too. That is one thing that communion helps us remember—we all have something different to give. When we share the bread and the cup we remember that we come together to be one family. The bread is special; it helps us remember. And the bread this morning will be extra special—because you helped with it!

A good way to end the time is to invite the children to "line out" the refrain to "One Bread, One Body" (United Methodist Hymnal #620). In the congregations where I used this, the children were sent out from worship for extended session. One congregation sent out some of the bread as it was shared in communion. In the other, the bread made a special appearance at a congregational dinner—the children each got a taste of *their* bread. (OIH)

21. Meditation and Prayer

There are those among us in the faith community who doubt and question whether it is appropriate for children to be present in and participate in worship. Perhaps this story will be a source of information and inspiration.

At the age of three, Laura Birch of First Christian Church in Orange, California, always stood in the pew with rapt attention. When the other young children came forward for the children's sermon and then went off to the nursery or lesson time, Laura would return to her pew and stand quietly so that she could see all of the service and hear it and maybe learn as much as possible. She was always attentive and well behaved, and a grand listener. From Laura there was no squirming or wiggling, just plain intense observation.

One day, while spending time with her grandmother, she was overheard in an important session with her dolls and stuffed animals. Lined up neatly on the den sofa sat a congregation of quiet and rapt congregants. Laura stood in front of them, leading them, from memory, in the practice of the words she knew so well:

"The body of Christ, broken for you. The blood of Christ, poured out for you."

And in the conclusion of her practice of the words she knew so well, Laura added her own benediction: "Ladies and gentlemen...God loves you!" Amen.

Prayer:

Creator God, we come as children today to feed upon your holy Word and promise. Comfort us as we partake of this loaf and this cup; remind us of our duty: to live in wholeness and unity of faith and, like our children, to open our hearts and minds to your healing Spirit. Help us today with new and childlike spirit to recapture the hope of the resurrection and the promise of life and life eternal. Strengthen us with this loaf and cup and feed us with your constant love. And dear God, teach us to share it, freely and joyfully as children. We pray with all certainty that we will see thy Kingdom come, through Jesus Christ our savior. Amen.

(CH)

22. Prayer for the Cup
(Thanksgiving for Children)

God of changes,
We rejoice this morning
in celebrating our children:
Their passage from one year to the next
is marked by us today
in their passage from one class to the next.

Yet, in their growth,
they also grow away from us:
They confront us with the uncertainty
of an unknown future,
With our frantic desire
to cling to what we have,
to control time itself.

We give thanks,
God of children,
that the parables of Jesus
offer us a kin-dom
not ruled by Father Time,
where surprise is our proper portion.

Let the rich liquid of this cup
tell us the story anew!
Let its stillness awaken our desire for constancy,
not stasis.
Let its flow and movement add grace to our struggle
with time and change.

We find your Spirit
in this bread and cup
and, especially, in the faces
of our children.
For their sake,
we commit ourselves
to your work,
That the prophecy of peace
may indeed be ours.

(CC)

23. Communion Prayer
(For a Wedding)

Lord of love, as we celebrate this marriage today, and come to have communion together, we remember that great wedding feast to come when your church will be united with you in the fulfillment of God's reconciliation. As _____ and _____ come before you to share in their first communion together in the blessing of their relationship, we pray this bond will resemble the love you have for your church: never ending and always full of grace. Let this bread and wine symbolize the love of Christ so that they may know that when life is not easy, they can cast their burden upon you and count on you to answer the questions they may have in times of struggle. Help them to recognize the celebration in this feast of love. For this celebration is a celebration of the love Christ gives to us that we may celebrate his love with one another. May this bread of life and cup of salvation bless each of those who partake and shine upon us the love of God. For it is in Christ's name we pray. Amen.

(LRL)

24. Meditation

One summer while serving as camp counselor at church camp, I learned a whole new meaning of communion that can only come from the mouths of babes. Fifth and sixth graders can help adults comprehend the vastness of God's love in simplistic ways. My co-counselor and I took our troop to the waterfront, where vespers were regularly held at the foot of a cross made from Carolina pines. I asked a simple question of these young Disciples: "What is communion?" Some looked at one another; then one hand went up from a young boy, who responded, "Isn't it like a big family reunion?"

What a brilliant concept! When you think about it, communion is a family reunion. Family reunions are known for seeing wonderful aunts, uncles, grandparents, cousins, nieces, and nephews! We reacquaint ourselves, finding out who we're related to, eat good food, and celebrate the whole day just because we're a family.

At communion, we see all those wonderful people of God: those who helped us with a kind word during a difficult time;

the CWF group that has their circle meeting in our home; the Chi Rho youth; the elder who helped in our pastor's class; the minister who baptized us. You know them and they're all around. You know their faces and smiles. They're your church family. We know we are related simply by the name of the one who gave us the love of God in a new way. We celebrate this family reunion on a special day, at every Sabbath. The family reunion begins now. Won't you come and celebrate our family's name? Our name? Christian.

(LRL)

25. Prayer of Thanksgiving and Invocation

God of love, with Christians in every time and place
we give thanks for your love.
Day after day, through all of life,
you care for us beyond anything that
we deserve or earn.

Empowered by your love, we promise to love you
with all our heart, mind, soul, and strength,
and to love one another as we love ourselves.
All of this we do because of Jesus Christ
whom we remember and proclaim
with these gifts of bread and wine.
Of his own free will he came to live among us
so that we could know your love more completely.
He accepted death upon the cross
to show that love can never be overcome.

By your Holy Spirit
be present and active in this holy meal
that Jesus' own words may be fulfilled:
My body given for you.
My blood of the covenant poured out for you.
Holy God, as we receive this sacrament of love
into our own selves,
help us to live sacrificially and joyfully
in all that we do.
We ask this through Jesus Christ,
with you and the Holy Spirit,
one God for ever and ever. Amen.

(KW)

26. Communion Liturgy

Offertory Prayer:

God of wind and fire,
Your Spirit moves within us as we worship
and among us in our fellowship.
Your passion for all creation stirs our pride in belonging
and evokes humility before our responsibility.
We offer these gifts out of the abundance we enjoy.
We pray their use for the fulfillment of Jesus' ministry,
especially among our sisters and brothers not so blessed.
In the name of him who taught us to pray:

Lord's Prayer (in unison)

Dialogue:

Leader: The Lord be with you.

People: AND ALSO WITH YOU.

Leader: Lift up your hearts.

People: WE LIFT THEM TO THE LORD.

Leader: Let us give thanks to the Lord our God.

People: IT IS RIGHT TO GIVE OUR THANKS AND PRAISE.

Communion Prayer:

Ever-present God, the one who has been from the beginning:
thanksgiving flows from our hearts to our lips
when we remember what our people have witnessed.
We were there when you guided and taught a generation
through your servant Moses.
We were there when Jesus asked,
"Do you want to be made well?"
We were there with the women who found the
empty Easter tomb.
We were there when the rush of a mighty wind
filled a Pentecostal room.
With awe and reverence we set this table with bread and wine
at Jesus' command and accept his invitation to commune in
your presence.
We remember that he took a loaf of bread, and when he had
given thanks, he broke it and gave it to them, saying,
"This is my body, which is given for you.
Do this in remembrance of me."
And he did the same with the cup after supper, saying,

"This cup that is poured out for you is the new covenant in my blood."
Come, Holy Spirit, in power and in blessing. Amen.
Communion

Post-communion Prayer:

> Gracious God, we who have gathered here today
> now leave this table well fed.
> With bread, our strength is renewed
> for inviting others to come into your presence.
> Having drunk the wine, our resolve is strengthened
> to serve all for whom Christ died.
> Creator, mold us;
> Redeemer, fill us;
> Spirit, use us. Amen. (MAP)

27. Prayer for the Bread
(Psalm 139:1–12; Luke 10:25–37)

Holy and ever-present God,
We give thanks for your inexhaustible love!
We run from you:
We cannot bear to see the holy
in ourselves.
We run from neighbor:
Not just the maimed and dying
on our every city's streets,
But even from our friends and loved ones—
Like you, they know us too well,
our holiness and our demons.

Yes, you, O God,
you know us body and soul.
And, in the person of Jesus,
you tell a story of glory,
written in our every weakness and strength.
Let us eat now the bread of presence!
Let us eat now the bread of constancy and steadfast love!
Let us eat now the broken bread
of wholeness!

Open our hearts to your Spirit,
our eyes and hands to each other.
Make us holy neighbors!

(CC)

28. Meditation
(1 Corinthians 11; 14)

Minister: Let us listen to an exchange between the Corinthian church and the apostle Paul. A faction in the Corinthian church says:

Elder: "The women should keep silence in the churches, for they are not permitted to speak, but should be subordinate, as even the law says. If there is anything they desire to know, let them ask their husbands at home. For it is shameful for a woman to speak in church."

Minister: To which Paul replied:

Elder: "What! Did the word of God originate with you, or are you the only ones it has reached?" (1 Corinthians 14:34–36 RSV).

Minister:

This faction within the Corinthian congregation assumed their theological privilege to judge everyone within the congregation—that even as the law says, all men should be circumcised, and that everyone should keep the Mosaic dietary regulations. They further believed that since men were created first, they were closer to God and therefore were to rule women in the home, in the church, and in the world. Therefore, women were to be veiled (1 Corinthians 11:5–10) and silent in church.

But Saint Paul was bewildered and shocked by their contentious illusions of self-importance. "What! Did the word of God originate with you, or are you the only ones it has reached?" The word of God is not wrought by human hand nor is it a commodity to be regulated by the self-appointed self-righteous.

Neither is this table a commodity bought, owned, and regulated by any congregation or denomination. No one, no person or group within the church, has the theological authority to exclude another from this holy meal. The bread and wine are symbolic gifts of forgiveness and reconciliation to God's people. The grace of God is not ours to control, but simply to offer on behalf of the Lord Jesus Christ to all who would come.

(DOS)

29. Communion Prayer
(Zechariah 7:1–10; Luke 5:33–35)

God of prophecy
and of parable—
We give thanks that your word
comes to us
in so many ways:

In the demanding tones of the prophet,
you compose the song
of right worship,
measured in justice and compassion.

With the elusive melody of parable,
you teach us the times
of feasting and of fasting,
when to drink the old wine,
and when the new.

We believe that the Spirit that binds us
and makes us church
marks the presence
of the bridegroom among us,
that this feast we keep
is indeed your feast
and not our own.

Bearing this witness,
we drink this wine—
the new wine
that surpasses even the old—
and commit your church once more
to the widow—and the single mother,
to the orphan—and the abused child,
to the stranger—all whom we regard
as different from ourselves,
to the poor—and to changing the structures
that create poverty.

In the name of Jesus we pray.

(CC)

30. Meditation and Prayer

Perhaps the most decisive part of Jesus' ministry—and certainly one of the most controversial to church leaders of the day—was his habit of choosing unusual people (some thought them the worst of people) to sit down at the table to share and to eat with. During the course of his ministry he ate with tax collectors, sinners, outcasts of all sorts. Sitting at the table with him, people learned and grew in their understanding of God. They were transformed people.

It was no different the night he shared the Last Supper with his disciples, for they too were sinners. Even Judas, who would betray him later that same night, was included in the meal. It is no different today—for Jesus invites us all to come just as we are, sinners or saints, rich or poor, weak or strong. The only requirement is that we believe in him. And as we sup together, we, too, like those people, have the opportunity to realize our faith, to experience new life and new possibilities, and to become changed people so that we may go forth from this place empowered by the Holy Spirit to be God's people and to do God's will in our world.

Prayer:

We come before you, dear God, filled with a sense of gratitude for your gifts of love and grace. We are never more aware of those gifts than at this moment when we gather in communion. We would remember, God, that the disciples were ordinary people, just as we are ordinary people, changed by their response to your redeeming love and that we, too, are offered that same redemptive love, if we will but accept it and respond to it.

Teach us, we pray, to live both responsively and responsibly in the new freedom of forgiveness and in the reality of your love, which we celebrate through these symbols of loaf and cup. Help us to remember, not just here at the table, but in every hour of every day. Amen.

(MB)

31. Prayer for the Bread

Incarnate God!
You are the lover of the earth
and all that dwells therein.
You have clothed the lily in splendor.
You mark the arc of each sparrow in the sky.
You stretch out your arms to us,
and bring us close,
in the embrace of mother and child.

We give thanks that the wonder of your love
allows *us* to love in more fully human ways:
able not only to rejoice with the rejoicing,
but to grieve with the grieving;
responsive not only to the hurts of those
close to us,
but also to the suffering of millions
we do not know.

In this broken bread this morning,
we remember every body broken,
and every broken heart.
We remember also, O God,
that in Jesus Christ
our brokenness became your own.

And we claim the promise of the Spirit
that the human journey does not end here,
but in the body restored.

We are your church!
Create us in your image!
Make us the sign
of your peace
on earth.

(CC)

32. Meditation and Prayer
(For World Communion Sunday)

On the first Sunday of the year 1992, I stood in the pulpit of the colored congregation of the Coronationville Congregational Church in Johannesburg, South Africa. I looked out at the people, unprepared as I was to preach the word of the Lord in this place. I was even more unprepared to note that all of the people out there looked just like the folks in my home congregation. I could not speak at first, overcome with a sense of betrayal. Here I was in a place, an unsafe place, thousands of miles from home, in a land where prejudice and ignorance and hatred bind people into lives of separation. Here I was standing up before a community of faith, in a packed sanctuary on the first Sunday of the year, seeing with my own eyes hundreds of people who looked just like me. My fear gave way to shame. I knew, again, that nowhere on the face of this planet can human beings who have faith, who live in faith, who celebrate in faith their hope for renewal of life…nowhere can we be separated from the love of God, or from one another as the people of God. No one can separate us.

The service proceeded, much like my own at home. And being the first Sunday of the year and the month, the morning ended with communion. I was asked to celebrate.

I stood at the front of the sanctuary with tears in my eyes and the loaf and the cup in my hand. It was a Sunday morning that pushed me into the practice of faith and the memory of hope that is the promise to all of God's people in all places at all times. This time "World Communion Sunday" was in the world of the people of God who live in a place that is the antithesis of God's plan for the unity of all people. But for all time, and on all Sundays where there is communion, I will know that around the table are gathered here and there all people of faith regardless of distance or man-made barriers.

> For I am convinced that neither death, nor life, nor angels, nor rulers, nor things present, nor things to come, nor powers, nor height, nor depth, nor anything else in all creation, will be able to separate us from the love of God in Christ Jesus our Lord.
>
> (Romans 8:38–39)

Prayer:

God of all nations: forgive our constant testing of you. Help us to know you in all times and all places, and remind us that your Holy Spirit abides in all times and all places. Teach us as we partake of the common loaf and cup that your blessing is poured out for all people. Help us in each day, and at each feast of life, to feel your binding spirit, to know your forgiving blessing, and to touch the community of faith in all the earth, loving and embracing those whom we see and those whom we do not seek.

In participating in this meal, wrap your Spirit around each of us, that we in all places and in all situations may take nourishment and strength and hope from this table.

In all the world, in all times and places, call us together as we are here now, in the blessing of the loaf and the cup to be your Kingdom on all the earth.

In the name of Christ we pray. Amen.

(CH)

33. Meditation
(For World Communion Sunday)

Look what you hold in your hands! You received this bread and this cup from the deacons, who received it from the elders (and pastor), who received it as from the hands of Jesus Christ himself. In this meal, we join that first table of disciples, and with them we eat and drink. In this Communion, the doors of time itself are opened, and the centuries collapse back to that beginning. We share this bread and cup with all those who eat of it around the world today, and with all who have eaten of it throughout time. From church to tent to brush arbor to chapel to cathedral to catacomb to upper room, all of us have received this bread and cup from the hands of Christ. And we look forward to the time when we shall receive it anew in the glory of God's own realm. Let time be a barrier no more, and let us know ourselves before our Master, our Savior, our Friend. In his name, and in his love, let us join in true communion. Amen.

(DW)

34. Meditation and Prayer
(For World Communion Sunday)
(Ephesians 4:1–6)

Some time ago a group gathered in the basement of a church to watch slides fresh from a missionary trip to Africa. Seated on creaky chairs in a cavernous fellowship hall the faithful stifled yawns as they watched the videotaped images from far away flicker across the screen. There were scenes of African men gouging a well from the earth, beaded necklaces swinging with every effort. The timbers of anonymous walls were hoisted up against alien landscapes. In surreal order, the time-lapse photography of the videotape captured the building's completion. The walls were slapped together with wood and mud; bundles of grassy thatch were tied to the roof.

On the inside, the sights were just as strange. Turbaned women in exotic swirls of fabric swayed to unfamiliar music. Voices rose to chant in mysterious language. Bare feet stamped the earthen floors; dust glimmered in the morning light.

Suddenly, amidst all that was strange and alien, something familiar was beginning to happen. Men and women came forward from the crowd. The singing and clapping dropped to a rhythmic hum. The camera swept across the crowd and came to rest on a small table. Shiny trays filled with bread and juice shimmered in the African sun. The deacons lifted the trays and began to serve the faithful.

In a fellowship hall thousands of miles away, seated on creaky folding chairs, the faithful recognized the faithful. In this place today, we recognize the faithful who break bread in Christ's name.

Prayer:
God, we give you thanks for the richness of the world you have created. We see your image in the flash of dark eyes, in the glimmer of blond hair; we see your face in many colors and shapes. We hear your voice even in languages that we do not speak. We give you thanks for all the ways you make your presence known to us.

But even though we praise your name in many tongues, we praise the one Lord. We know that in you we have one common faith, one common life, one common hope. Thank you for binding us together in Jesus Christ.

As we gather at one table today, remind us of other tables. Let us see many hands breaking bread. Let us see many cups raised up for blessing. Remind us that this table knows no boundaries. Help us stretch it from one horizon to the other, with all the faithful gathered around it.

As we eat the bread and drink the cup, unite us in a new world vision. Fill us with the spirit of justice, strengthen us with wisdom to see the world with new eyes. Help us speak a word of life to this death-loving world. Help us join our hands together to push back the tyrants. Help us join hands to bring food to the hungry.

Bless this meal and all who share it. Unite us in one Lord, one faith, one baptism. In the name of Jesus Christ, who gives us new life, we pray. Amen.

(LSM)

35. Meditation/Children's Sermon
(For World Communion Sunday)

Materials Needed: Breads from a variety of cultures—perhaps a loaf of wheat bread, Mexican sweet bread, pitas, etc.—and juices from a number of climates—grape, apple, pineapple, mango, and coconut milk. To complete the world theme, pictures of worshiping communities from around the world or a set of small international flags might be displayed about the table, or a globe can be used.

Worship Setting: If possible, arrange a variety of breads and juices in different kinds of baskets and cups on the communion table. Surround the table with photos and/or flags from other countries.

Process: Invite the children to join you. You might say something like: "Today is a special Sunday for us. Today is World Communion Sunday. People all around the world in all different kinds of churches are getting together in worship, celebrating communion. Some years ago there was a Disciples minister named Jesse Bader. He worked with Christians from all over the world and he came up with a really great idea. He thought, 'Wouldn't it be neat if Christians all over the world could all choose one Sunday each year and plan on having communion on that day? It would be a way of remembering how *big* God's family really is—how many Christian sisters and brothers we have in Canada, in Mexico, in Northern

Ireland, in Zaire, in...(you might encourage them to name countries, too), etc.'

"Christians all over the world—all taking communion on the same day—and all remembering that we are all one body in Christ, all one family in God. World Communion Sunday is a way to remember that the church is much bigger than just us. And today we are remembering that by having breads and juices from around the world. Grapes cannot grow every place, so some people use juices from fruits they *can* grow. This morning, as we eat these different breads and drink these juices from all over the world, we will be having communion with our sisters and brothers in the church around the world."

Follow-up: The last time I used this sermon, the children found a surprise waiting for them in their room. A large table had been prepared for them as much like the one in the sanctuary as possible. All the breads and juices were laid out. Music from different countries played on tape and pictures and decorations from other countries filled the room. In short, we celebrated World Communion Sunday as an International Festival. Each child was able to taste the breads and juices she or he wanted, not as the Lord's Supper exactly, but as ways of learning how many different ways there are of having communion. This helped the children connect a bit with what was going on in "grown-up" worship as well as the international celebrations of the day. We played a singing game from France, sang a hymn from Africa ("Kum Ba Yah"), and closed the day with a big piñata.

(OIH)

36. Meditation

It takes an unseen circle of hands to prepare this supper laid out before us. Someone somewhere grew the wheat and reaped it. Someone somewhere made the bread. Someone else packaged and sold it to us for our use today. The juice for the cup took a similar path, from vineyard to processing plant to store to us. It took someone of our own church family here to come early and prepare this meal for us, to lay out the bread and fill the cup(s).

An unseen circle of hands has prepared our feast. Unseen too are the hands of God who has called us here, and who blesses us, sharing this feast of life with us. Now a new circle of hands will take these elements and distribute them to us, and our hands will join that circle as we take the bread, and take the cup. Seen and unseen, known and unknown, this circle of hands is united by this bread and this cup. For this circle of hands is the family of God; this circle of hands is the body of Christ.

(DW)

37. Prayer for the Cup
(In Time of War)

As we drink this cup of presence,
merciful God,
forebodings of absence
press upon us.

The absence wrought by war,
of person and of peace,
threatens to rend
the soul of your people,
to face us with the abyss
that denies all life.

Eyes blind, ears deaf,
lips sealed, hearts numb,
We still make our way
to this table—

Where we hear the story
of Jesus' death
and resurrection,
Where we see the eyes and touch the hand
of the person who passes us
this cup,
Where we feel and taste the wine
on our tongues—

And we give thanks
that in your mercy
our hearts can still open
to your presence,
Even in our shadowed valleys.

(CC)

38. Prayer for the Cup
(In Time of Global Conflict)

We come to this table as your children,
God of life,
Seeking in this familiar ritual
the peace and bonding that should be
at the center of every family.
And we come also
acknowledging our brokenness:
of self,
of family,
of world.

Some members of our family
seem so distant:
an estranged child,
a spiteful sibling,
a rejecting parent.
Some members,
in this time of trouble,
we even label "enemy":
your children in Baghdad
and the bunkers of Kuwait.
But the burden of brokenness
is not ours to bear alone:
in this cup of blood spilt,
where Jesus' humanity mingles with our own,
we find the promise of new life,
a new vision of family:
the unreconcilable are reconciled,
stranger becomes neighbor,
and we give thanks
for the inexpressible joy
of meeting you
in every person we greet.

(CC)

39. Prayer for the Bread
(For a Commitment Sunday, with unmet goals)

You have promised, O God,
that this loaf would always
be large enough!
And we give thanks
for the many times
it has fed a multitude!

Yet there are times in our communal life
when our faith has been small,
when we were sure
that the pieces of this body
were broken
into the smallest of crumbs,
and could spread no further.

And, especially in these times,
we give thanks
that you did not send your Son
to the well-fed or the saints;
for the poor and the sinners
Christ died.

On this Sunday,
when we, as the body of Christ,
gather to commit our substance
to the work of your Church,
generous God,
send your Spirit to remind us,
in the darkest days of the year,
your light comes!

And send us into the world,
knowing where your Son will be found:
in the hungry whom we feed,
in the naked we clothe.

Take away our fear:
your loaf will not fail!

(CC)

40. Meditation
(1 Corinthians 11:23–26)

I was teaching the pastor's class in my first church out of seminary when I heard my voice—*my* voice—say, "No, it's only a symbol."

My response was to Amy's question about communion. Amy was the star in the class, and she always had a question that would put me on the spot. This time she had said: "My friend goes to St. Francis Xavier (the local Catholic church). She says that they eat Christ's body and drink his blood for communion. Do we do that?" That's when I heard myself say, "No, it's only a symbol."

ONLY A SYMBOL. . . as though that made it somehow less than real. ONLY A SYMBOL. . . I had forgotten for the moment that symbols are the most powerful things we have. Indeed, we don't have them at all; they have us!

Remember the story of Lord Nelson sailing into Aboukir Bay with six colors flying so that even if five were shot away there would be one left to inspire his men? That flag was only a symbol.

Look at your left hand. That band of gold or silver that has worn a groove in your fourth finger reminds you of the one you love and by whom you are loved. Yet, it's only a symbol.

During Operation Desert Storm, on several car antennae and coat lapels I saw yellow or orange ribbons, a reminder to all of us of the common prayer that our men and women would soon return from distant lands. Yet the ribbon was only a symbol.

Of course, there are plenty of good reasons for giving up on symbols: they are not universally understood; their meanings are misappropriated by careless or venal people; they are constantly changing and they contribute to an "in group/out group" mentality of those who know the symbol and those who don't. (Don't take it from me; just ask your teenager what the latest hot words are.) All are good reasons for getting rid of symbols.

But a symbol wisely chosen and intelligently understood is the most powerful tool in the world. Symbols are what we use when words won't do the job. Either we can't find the right words, or the words we want to use get stuck on the lump in our throat. Then symbols become all-important...a single red rose...a carefully folded flag presented on behalf of a grateful nation at the conclusion of a simple, yet dignified ceremony...wildly pealing bells as the couple races down the church sidewalk through a shower of rice to their waiting car.

"Only a symbol." Dear God, what had I said?

After he had shared a meal with his disciples, Jesus took bread and wine, essentially the leftovers of the meal, elements that would grace the table three times a day in any household of his time, and he made them forever memorable. "When you eat the bread, when you drink the cup, remember me. Remember that you are freed from sin because I have taken it upon myself. Remember how much God loves you." Three times a day. Words from one who has the power to take the most ordinary elements of life and transform them so that they are unforgettable...transform them so that *he* is unforgettable.

Jesus takes the commonplace and transforms it into the extraordinary: water into wine, sickness into health, death into life, doubt into faith, a rag-tag band of fishers and tax collectors into disciples, us into more than we know we are. And the transformer and the transformation go on...patiently, tirelessly, ceaselessly.

Only a symbol? The truth, Amy, is that we live and die by symbols. So as we consider the symbol at the table before us, let us newly appropriate it as a celebration of Christ's transforming power.

(GR)

41. Meditation
(For Thanksgiving)

Around our Thanksgiving table there are significant special people bonded in that thing we call family. We get together as often as possible and cherish each other's company—and usually a meal. But first we give thanks to God.

It's like that here, too. We gather round this table as often as possible. It should be like a happy family in joyous reunion—truly cherishing each other. It should be a time of giving thanks to God. It should be the best of all Thanksgiving meals, for so it is.

We remember that on that night when Jesus gathered with the disciples in a meal of thanksgiving he took the bread. Let us give thanks.

(CDN)

42. Prayer for the Cup
(Zephaniah 3:1–9; 2 Timothy 4:6–8, 16, 18)

We give thanks, Righteous Judge,
that even in the city of oppressors
we hear your challenging word.

We give thanks
for this opportunity in worship
to confess the sin
in our easy assumption
that when things are going well for us,
you must be on our side.

And, here at this table,
we give most special thanks
for the life, death, and resurrection of Jesus,
through whom we learn the living relationship
of piety and justice;
who opens our eyes to the vision
of the lion lying down
with the lamb.

This cup we pour and consume
is ever refilled,
and our race toward righteousness and justice
is never run alone.

As your body,
we share your Spirit.
Judge us, God, this day.

(CC)

43. Prayer
(For All Saints' Day)

Holy God, the fountain from which all life springs
and the reservoir into which all life flows,
the beginning and fulfillment of life, we honor you.
With gratitude we remember the prophets and martyrs
of every age who lived by faith
and died in the confidence of your steadfast love.
Especially do we praise you for Jesus Christ
who by his zeal for the holy commonwealth
and its righteousness showed us how to live

and by his constant faithfulness against all odds
showed us how to die.
In Christ's own name we pray. Amen.

Merciful God, with this loaf and cup
we remember Jesus as he asked us to do.
By your Word and Holy Spirit bless your church
and this offering of bread and wine,
that Jesus' own words may be fulfilled:
>My body given for you.
>My blood of the covenant poured out for you.

We pray that in life and in death
we, like Jesus, will always be sustained by your love,
and that when the time comes we will be received
back into the eternity of life with you.
This we pray through the same Jesus Christ,
with you and the Holy Spirit,
one God for ever and ever. Amen.

(KW)

44. Meditation
(Hebrews 10:23–25)

On the farm we never used the word *guest*. We said we had
company. The root word for *company* refers to people who
share bread together. While we didn't usually eat bread with
company, we usually had refreshments. The word *company*
shares the same root as *companion*. Companions are those
whose lives intertwine and sustain us along our life's journey.
Sometimes our company (or companions) saw a dirty kitchen
floor or clothes all over the laundry room or toys scattered
everywhere but in the toy box. But as we visited together and
munched on snacks, there was no attempt to be better than
one another. There was no need to "put on airs." After all, this
was company: people we trusted and loved, who brightened
our lives, not because they were so important or outstanding,
but just because of their presence. These visits sustained us.

We are company who share the Lord's Supper together.
We are companions in worship, all equal with one another,
encouraging, sharing our stories of cares and laughter, our
lives intertwined by our faith journeys. Perhaps this is why

the writer with Hebrews reminds us not to forsake assembling together with one another. We all are sustained by the company of such companions.

As we gather around this table for God's refreshment, look around you to the companions whose presence sustains you. The presence of God is in our midst because the presence of the community of Jesus Christ, our companions along our faith journey, declares it to be so.

(BD)

The Table That
Walks with Us

The resources in this collection have challenged us to come to
the table ready to listen to the mystery of salvation spoken
in the act of communion. The table has witnessed to us of the
continuing presence of God's power into and throughout our
lives. The table not only talks to us, it walks with us into our
daily lives.

Stanley Hauerwas, in his book *The Peaceable Kingdom*,
argues that communion is an ethical act, for in the celebrating
of communion Christians "become part of Christ's kingdom"
(Hauerwas 108). This link between communion celebration
and ethical action is dramatically enacted by the Masai people
who symbolize the peace of Christ by a ritual passing of a
handful of grass from one to another prior to communion.
However, if someone or some group in the village refuses to
accept the grass as the sign of the peace of Christ, there is no
celebration of communion at the worship service. Hauerwas
explains, "the Masai understand well the relation between
their eucharistic celebration and the demand to be a holy
people, a peaceable people....The Eucharist is possible be-

121

cause they have become what they, and we, were meant to be: a people capable of passing grass" (111).

Paul said it in a slightly different way. Commenting on the inequity of food distribution among the Corinthians at the communion meal he writes, "Whoever, therefore, eats the bread or drinks the cup of the Lord in an unworthy manner will be answerable for the body and blood of the Lord" (1 Corinthians 11:27). Commenting on the church throughout the world today, Tissa Balasuriya states, "If the eucharistic celebration does not lead to commitment, to personal and societal liberation in a serious manner, then all these externals are a mere distraction, a dissipation of energy and a lessening of the real meaning of the Eucharist" (Balasuriya 21).

The table that walks with us challenges our understanding of the relation between God and the church and between the church and the wider world. Transforming the communion meditations and prayers to witness to God's abiding presence is a powerful means of transforming the church's self-understanding and witness to the world (Proctor-Smith 30). Catherine LaCugna notes that the word *communion* means shared life. "Persons who exist together in true communion share happiness, share hope, share suffering, share responsibility." In communion we "receive the Body of Christ and go forward to love and serve God and the people of God's household" ("The Practical Trinity" 681–682).

The communing church is challenged to walk with God, sharing the good news of God's transforming power and presence, which works into and through our lives toward just relations in the world. This is the good news of the gospel, for in Christ God is reconciling the world. It is witnessing to the God who freely makes a covenant with Israel, the God who lovingly enters the world in Jesus of Nazareth, the God who longs for a mutual relation with us in the Spirit. It is the radical realization that God's presence is in mutual, loving, and free relation with creation.

In the breaking of bread we are transformed by the presence of God to be the body of Christ, transforming life into free, inclusive communities. In the image of God humanity is created as male and female, not as self-focused individuals but as persons in relationship. As Christians strive toward perfecting the image of God in their lives, they are called to build communities that mirror the mutual relationality of the gospel. As these communities strive toward the good of the individual in relation to the whole, they will be free. As these communities strive to treasure and include all persons, realizing their inherent contribution to the whole, they will be loving.

While Christians will continue to "see in a mirror, dimly," they can proclaim the hope of the resurrection that they are being transformed into the body of Christ. Our hope is that "no longer will Christians trudge single file into the fray clutching bread crumbs and a trickle of juice. God's people will flock into the world, bearing whole loaves and brimming flasks. We will carry the saving bread of mercy into a starving world" (May 30).

Key to Contributors

AP	Allene Parker
BD	Beverly Dale
CC	Claudia Camp
CDN	Charlotte D. Nabors
CE	Curt Ehrmantraut
CH	Claudia Highbaugh
CKC	Christine K. Chenoweth
DC	Diane Caughron
DOS	David Odell-Scott
DW	Drea Walker
GR	Gregory Russell
JF	Jacquelyn Foster
JM	Jane McAvo
KEW	Karen E. Warren
KLS	Karen Leigh Stroup
KT	Ken Taliaferro
KW	Keith Watkins
LOS	Lauren Odell-Scott
LPR	Linda Patrick-Rosebrock
LRL	Lydia R. Land
LSM	L. Susan May
MAP	Mary Anne Parrott
MB	Marsha Bishop
NCP	Nancy Claire Pittman
OIH	O.I. Cricket Harrison
SM	Sandra Messick
SP	Stephanie Paulsell
SW	Steve Webb
VL	Virgina Liggett

Works Cited

Balasuriya, Tissa. *The Eucharist and Human Liberation.* Maryknoll, New York: Orbis Press, 1979.

Brock, Rita Nakashima. *Journeys by Heart: A Christology of Erotic Power.* New York: Crossroad, 1988.

Harrison, Beverly Wildung. *Making the Connections: Essays in Feminist Social Ethics.* Ed. Carol S. Robb. Boston: Beacon Press, 1985.

Hauerwas, Stanley. *The Peaceable Kingdom: A Primer in Ethics.* South Bend, Indiana: University of Notre Dame Press, 1983.

Johnson, Elizabeth. *She Who Is: The Mystery of God in a Feminist Theological Discourse.* New York: Crossroad, 1992.

LaCugna, Catherine Mowery. *God for Us: The Trinity and Christian Life.* San Francisco: Harper Press, 1991.

LaCugna, Catherine Mowery. "The Practical Trinity." *Christian Century.* July 15–22, 1992: 678–682.

May, L. Susan. "Beyond Schizophrenia." *Disciples Theological Digest* 7:1 (1992): 27–31.

Proctor-Smith, Marjorie. *In Her Own Rite: Constructing Feminist Liturgical Tradition.* Nashville: Abingdon Press, 1990.

Schaberg, Jane. *The Illegitimacy of Jesus: A Feminist Theological Interpretation of the Infancy Narratives.* San Francisco: Harper and Row, 1987.

Sykes, Stephen. "The Sacraments." *Christian Theology: An Introduction to Its Traditions and Tasks.* 2nd ed. Eds. Peter C. Hodgson and Robert H. King. Philadelphia: Fortress Press, 1985: 274–301.

The Gifts We Bring. Indianapolis: Church Finance Council, n.d.

Watkins, Keith. *The Feast of Joy: The Lord's Supper in Free Churches.* St. Louis: Bethany Press, 1977.

Wilson-Kastner, Patricia. *Faith, Feminism and the Christ.* Philadelphia: Fortress Press, 1983.